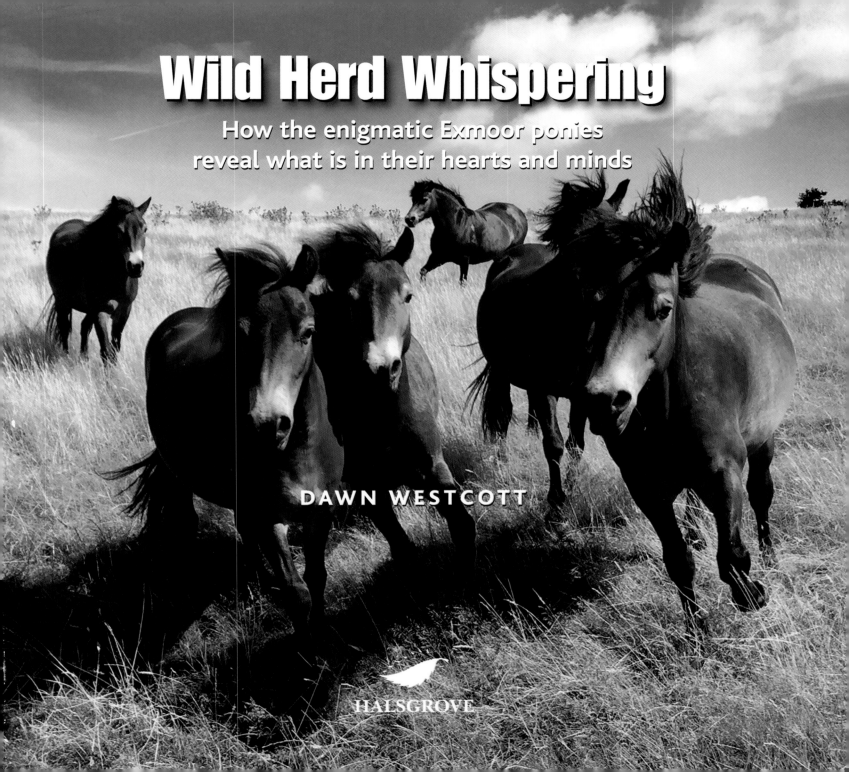

Wild Herd Whispering

How the enigmatic Exmoor ponies reveal what is in their hearts and minds

DAWN WESTCOTT

HALSGROVE

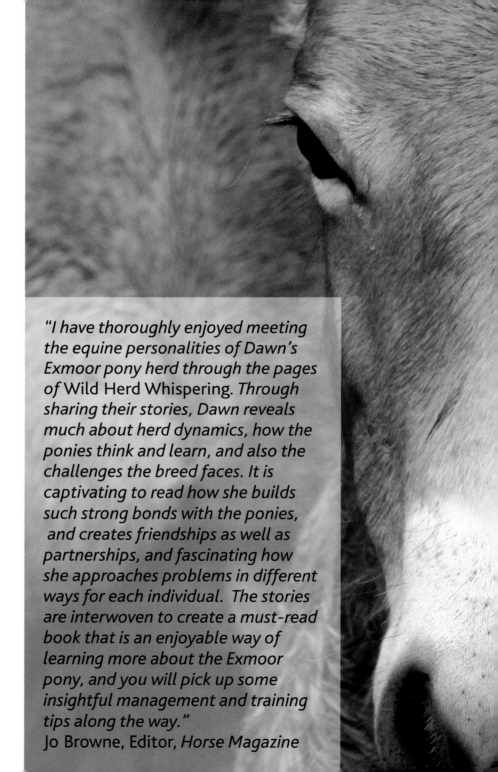

First published in Great Britain in 2017
Copyright © Dawn Westcott 2017
© The photographers in respect of their
individual contributions

British Library Cataloguing-in-Publication Data
A CIP record for this title is available from the
British Library

ISBN 978 0 85704 318 4

HALSGROVE

Halsgrove House, Ryelands Business Park,
Bagley Road, Wellington, Somerset TA21 9PZ
Tel: 01823 653777   Fax: 01823 216796
email: sales@halsgrove.com

Part of the Halsgrove group of companies
Information on all Halsgrove titles is
available at: www.halsgrove.com

Printed and bound by Parksons Graphics, India

"I have thoroughly enjoyed meeting the equine personalities of Dawn's Exmoor pony herd through the pages of Wild Herd Whispering. *Through sharing their stories, Dawn reveals much about herd dynamics, how the ponies think and learn, and also the challenges the breed faces. It is captivating to read how she builds such strong bonds with the ponies, and creates friendships as well as partnerships, and fascinating how she approaches problems in different ways for each individual. The stories are interwoven to create a must-read book that is an enjoyable way of learning more about the Exmoor pony, and you will pick up some insightful management and training tips along the way."*
Jo Browne, Editor, *Horse Magazine*

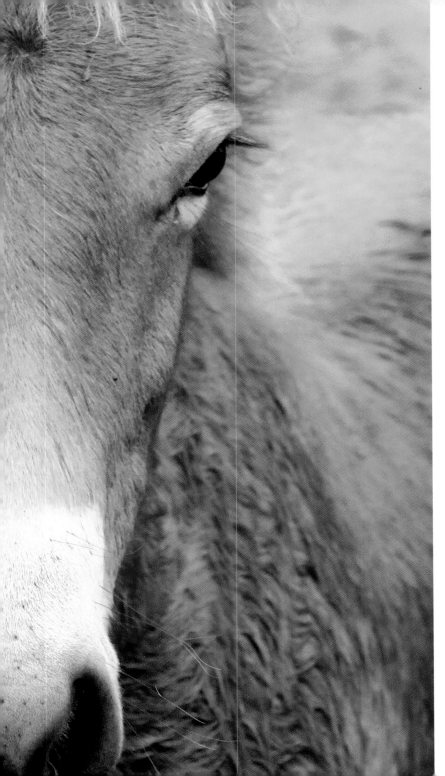

Contents

Nick and Dawn Westcott with Monsieur Chapeau.

THIS BOOK IS DEDICATED TO:

I am dedicating this book to my husband Nick Westcott. Without his love, wisdom, generosity, help, compassion, resilience and integrity - none of this would have happened. We've faced some tiresome obstruction in endeavouring to save the lives and find good opportunities for Exmoor ponies and improve their welfare and status. Nick has remained a rock in the ocean throughout and he also values and facilitates research and development into the socialisation, handling and management of the ponies, to help them enjoy happier and more fulfilling lives off the moor. I am also dedicating this book to our beautiful foundation mare Maisie (Smarty Pants) for the light and wisdom she has brought to our lives.

Thanks & Acknowledgements

Dawn would like to thank the following people
and organisations for their help, support and encouragement:

To everyone who has helped and supported our work and in particular Heather Williams, Sue Byrne, Millie Ker, June Eckhart, Melanie Maddocks, Peter Hotchkiss, Peter Green, Annette Barrett and Amelia Phillips, Alyson Govier and Clive Ponsford. Thanks also to The Moorland Exmoor Pony Breeders Group (MEPBG) members, Exmoor National Park Authority, the National Trust Holnicote Estate and the North Devon National Trust.

Photographers – Marc Lubetzki, Martin Buschmann, Dawn Westcott, Nick Westcott, Millie Ker, Alysoun Sharpe, Alyson Govier, Naomi Gubb-Fradgley, Gareth Latham, Christina Williams, Deborah Sheppard, Rebecca de Mendonca

Other books by Dawn Westcott:
Wild Pony Whispering – real-life story of orphaned, starving wild-born foal Monsieur Chapeau who showed us how to tame the wild ponies of Exmoor. ISBN 978 0 85704 276 7

Wild Stallion Whispering – real-life story of unwanted wild-born foal Bear and his amazing journey from the moor to world champion. ISBN 978 0 85704 293 4

For more information about Nick and Dawn Westcott's work with Exmoor ponies, the Exmoor Pony Project and Holtball Herd 11 Exmoor ponies, please visit www.WildPonyWhispering.co.uk

Chapter One

Lady of the Moor

Life is about to change dramatically for one tiny, very late born foal

On a bitingly cold December day, wind and rain lashed at the team of Exmoor farmers as they met high up on Molland Moor to round up the semi-feral Exmoor ponies. With around 1700 acres of bleakly beautiful moorland wilderness to cover, there was no telling how long it would take. A small group headed out on horseback and quad bikes, while others set up the handling pens. After a while, some bright mealy muzzles appeared on the horizon and the ponies cascaded across the moor to where we waited at White Post. Thankfully, they were relatively easy to bring in and were soon contained in the pens – ready to separate and wean the foals.

Both mares and foals were understandably agitated, staring and starting anxiously as they viewed the people surrounding them. While the older mares knew it was likely they would now lose their foals, the bewildered foals had no idea what was happening. In the midst of this medley stood a tiny very late-born foal – only a few weeks old. Instead of hiding behind the mares, the foal caught my eye, standing proud with poise and courage and curiously contemplating the handling team. However, semi-feral foals born this late, well outside of the normal breeding season can face the bleakest future.

The Molland Moor pony gathering.

Opposite: The little late-born foal with her dam and herd.

7

Molland Moor mares and foals waiting in the pens.

Moorland farming in the upland areas is notoriously hard and pragmatic decisions have to be made about livestock. 'Horse colts' (male foals) must come off the moor after gathering, because by the time the herd is brought in the following year, they may have started covering mares. With strict breeding programmes, only approved registered Exmoor stallions are permitted to run with the mares. 'Mare colts' (filly foals) are sometimes returned to the herd to replace older mares, or they may be offered for sale. It is not easy to find homes for the semi-feral foals, no matter how lovely, and it's almost impossible to find people willing to take on the care and expense of a very young, late born foal – who will need a considerable amount of mare replacement milk, costing over £100 a bag. So unfortunately, some of the foals can face being culled, particularly the colts.

As the ponies were directed through the handling shute, I continued to glance at the tiny foal. Sometimes spinning around with the others, the foal nevertheless always turned to face the handlers, staring up at them enquiringly as if to ask, 'What on earth is going on?' – and showing an incredible self-possession. My heart went out to the little creature.

The Molland ponies have not been pedigree registered for some years, which means that the foals can no longer be entered into the Exmoor Pony stud book – as there is no upgrading system to enable them to rejoin the pedigree breeding gene pool. With Exmoor ponies being an endangered breed, and the tiny free-living population on Exmoor itself numbering under 500 ponies, the long-standing and authentic 'true moorland type' Molland Moor ponies are nevertheless important. However, the prospect of no pedigree registration for most if not all of the foals was going to make it even harder to find good homes for them.

It had not been the intention to breed from the Molland mares this past year, but two registered Exmoor stallions belonging to a herd owner elsewhere on Exmoor had broken out from their enclosure, onto Molland Moor, and covered the mares. The Molland herd owner, the Dart family, along with the Williams family of the Molland Estate, are members of the Moorland Exmoor Pony Breeders Group (MEPBG) which is working to improve the welfare, management and opportunities for Exmoor ponies on Exmoor. This includes involvement in the Exmoor Pony DNA Whole Genome Project, which aims to map the entire genetic make-up of the Exmoor pony. It is hoped that this pioneering new research will provide a way of establishing the purity of ponies outside the stud book and a route to re-introducing them to the pedigree breeding gene pool.

As the weaning of the foals continued in rain, wind and mud, one of the handlers caught hold of the tiny foal and called across that it was a 'horse colt', the local Exmoor term for a male. My heart sank. There was now no possibility of the foal remaining with his mother for the winter. So the brave little chap was bundled through the pens and into the trailer with the other older colts. The foal's mother retreated into the group of mares. There had been no need to pair them up because the little colt did not have a future.

'Can't we do something?' I asked my husband Nick, my eyes welling up. He looked at me.

'No Dawn, you need to forget about him and concentrate on the other foals. Remember what you're helping to save.'

I felt dreadful, but there was a job to be done and we continued to help sort out the herd. Soon, the mares were released back out onto the moor and the foals were taken to the farm in trailers. The MEPBG team would return to inspect them in a few days. The aim was for the fillies to remain with the herd, but a question mark hung over the fate of all of the colts. Their future was very uncertain, but not as uncertain as the tiny late born foal who without milk could not survive anyway. It was clear he would shortly be humanely despatched.

My eyes welled up again as we drove away.

'Can't we do something about that tiny foal – he's so perfect and I was so sure it was a filly.' I said.

My husband shook his head, just a little regretfully. I knew his was the voice of reason and that forgetting about the little foal was the sensible thing to do. We already had a large number of Exmoor ponies at home in our Exmoor Pony Project, with resources stretched to the limits. Nursing an extremely late-born unregisterable colt foal with bags of expensive mare replacement milk was a crazy idea. It was already going to be a challenge to find homes for the larger, older colts.

After picking up some supplies, we arrived back at our farm well into the evening, tired and chilled through from standing in the rain and cold all day. After we'd seen to the animals and I'd put a meal on the table, I simply couldn't contain my feelings about the foal.

'Nick, I can't stop thinking about that tiny foal. Do you not think it's just what our foal project is for? He's got no chance at all without our help. He's such a nice foal and almost definitely sired by one of the pedigree stallions that ran with the mares last year. He has their distinct "stamp" all about him.'

The two stallions had sadly since been euthanased and as their owner wasn't a member of our breeders group, we hadn't had the opportunity to try and re-home them. So these unplanned Molland foals were their very last progeny.

So tiny, the foal was only five weeks old.

Below: Arriving at Holt Ball to meet the big herd.

Bottom: Meeting the other ponies.

It must have been my expression because Nick rolled his eyes, sighed and picked up the phone. Somewhat embarrassed, he asked if the little foal was still alive.

'Well it will need some milk so we'd better come over and get it now,' he said. 'I know, I know. Yes, that's the one we want.'

Fortified with a flask of coffee, we hitched up the trailer and drove back to Molland late into the night. We were greeted with wry smiles as William Dart and his son Richard showed us to the barn where the colt foals were all settled and eating haylage. While the larger colts shied away, there standing firm and staring intently at us was the tiny foal. 'What's going on now?' he seemed to say. He must have been hungry and very tired but he faced us, four square, as proud as anything. I felt a lump in my throat. Being so tiny, it was easy for Nick and Richard to scoop the foal into a bear hug and half walk, half carry him to the trailer where he walked up inside – a tiny scrap of a foal making the stock trailer look huge. He gave out a determined whinny. Such spirit. Everyone was smiling. I felt a huge sense of relief that we had come back for him.

Back at our farm, we decided the foal should spend the night safely contained in the pony handling pens. These were set up inside a large barn, where our big herd of Exmoor ponies and three Arabian horses migrated in and out as they wished. This meant the ponies could come in and meet the foal and we felt that being alone would be far more frightening for him than meeting some strange ponies. When the herd drifted in, it was two year old Monsieur Chapeau — himself rescued as a starving, orphaned foal — who came straight up to the pen and the tiny foal sniffed noses with him before greeting the others. It was now well into the early hours and there was no way we could get mare replacement milk. We tried the foal on both lambs milk and ordinary milk with no luck.

'We'll get some mare replacement milk from the vet first thing in the morning,' said Nick.

Of course, being December, the milk proved to be like hen's teeth, but our vets had a small supply and a breeder in Devon had a little more, both kindly driven over by our friend June Eckhart. A larger order was placed with a feed supplier but it would take a day or two to arrive. The foal showed no interest in drinking from a bottle and in some despair, I poured some into a feed bucket — remembering the story of the two week old orphaned Herd 423 foal, Que Sera Sera (told in *Wild Pony Whispering*), who had preferred a bucket to a bottle. This proved to do the trick and the foal was soon drinking with enthusiasm. A great relief as we could now avoid bottle feeding which is not ideal.

Perhaps being so tiny and brave, and despite the trauma of being weaned so early, the foal was surprisingly friendly and easy to touch and allowed me to stroke the rump and gently pull aside the tail. To my delight, I saw she was indeed a filly! In the hustle and bustle of the pens, a mistake had been made, which is not uncommon.

First steps to gaining trust.

While we would have given a 'horse colt' just the same level of care, this was a real bonus. Here we had a beautiful little filly, with the quality stamp of one or other of the lovely pedigree stallions and out of a beautiful Molland mare. The foal was a prime candidate to benefit from the Genome Project and eventual purity testing, and there would be a strong case for her and her progeny to be re-introduced into the stud book through an upgrading system, if such a thing could be established. But stud book or no stud book, here was a very nice moorbred Exmoor filly whose Molland Moor genetics were important.

'Should she go back out onto the moor with her mother?' I said to Nick. We looked at the tiny little foal and discovered a large area of nasty rainscald on her back. Already December, with a long, cold, wet winter ahead, a question mark hung over her chances of survival out on one of the toughest moors of Exmoor.

'With the rain we've been having,' said Nick, 'I'm not sure she'd do very well out there and some of the mares had yearlings on them too. It would try her.'

'She's likely to be the last ever filly foal by one of those two stallions,' I said. 'She needs to survive and she's done a fantastic job so far. We'll have to do the best we can with her here.'

The filly needed a name and we chose Martha, which means 'an independent thinking lady'. So Lady Martha of Molland Moor would stay at Holt Ball. It was very unfortunate that she had been parted from her mother so soon, but she had survived. Now we had to help her thrive.

Chapter Two

Helping Hooves

Monsieur Chapeau and the herd show us what to do

When he was only about four months old, in early 2014 Monsieur Chapeau had been found alone in a wooded coombe, high up on the Dunkery Commons of Exmoor, starving and with pneumonia. He had somehow become separated from his mother and herd and it was thought unlikely he'd survive. But we nursed him back to health and he has since matured into a gorgeous, strapping Exmoor pony and plays an invaluable role in our herd.

When little Lady Martha arrived, Monsieur Chapeau made it very clear that he wanted to befriend her and he was soon able to spend some time with her in her pen and in the main barn area when the rest of the herd was out. Some months before, he had shown the same desire to nurture Lady Molly of Molland Moor, when she too had arrived as a late born foal. Interestingly, Lady Molly also came forward from the herd to befriend Lady Martha. Perhaps she remembered what it was like being introduced into the herd and wanted to help – and perhaps she recognised a fellow Molland Moor sibling?

Lady Martha with 'Wilson' the Spacehopper.

Monsieur Chapeau spending time with Lady Martha.

Another enormous help for Lady Martha was 'Wilson' the Spacehopper. I'd been playing with the ponies with giant balls and spacehoppers and I thought Lady Martha might appreciate something to push around and amuse herself with in her pen. She took a particular shine to the red spacehopper – which was almost as large as her. When its handles rolled onto the floor, it stopped moving and rocked back towards her. I could see that this 'response' from the spacehopper was comforting to Lady Martha – there was communication between them. She clearly adored 'Wilson', named after the volleyball that kept Tom Hanks company in Castaway – and she often slept right next to 'him'.

What about the other Molland foals?

Not long after the Molland gathering, we and Rex Milton (owner of moorland Herd 23), returned to carry out an MEPBG inspection of the filly and colt foals. The fillies would return to the herd the following spring and to our delight, it was confirmed that Ben and Christina Williams, of the Molland Estate, had agreed to take the colt foals for conservation grazing. Their future was safeguarded. It was a very good outcome.

Opposite: Lady Martha settling into her new home.

Lady Martha takes matters into her own hands

With Lady Martha now happily drinking the mare replacement milk, it was clear that she couldn't live in the pen day after day. While some people may keep a small foal stabled over the winter, we knew this would be pretty lonely and frustrating for an animal used to the freedom of the moor. We could let her stretch her legs and canter around the large barn when the herd was out – and sometimes interact with her new chums Monsieur Chapeau and Lady Molly – but we ideally had to work out a way for her to go outside too. The logistics made it tricky because our large herd of over twenty ponies and horses all migrate in and out of the barn to the pasture. It was inconceivable to think that this tiny five week old foal could run with the herd. Or could she?

After a few days, Lady Martha took matters into her own hands and quite frankly, frightened the life out of me.

I went out to the barn first thing that morning with her breakfast milk, only to find an empty pen and an empty barn. Rushing to examine the pen's gate, I was surprised to find it firmly shut. No animal could open this stock gate. Perplexed I searched around the pen for some breach or way she could have escaped. It was all secure. Then I looked at the gaps between the pen railings and thought, 'Surely not?' Lady Martha would have had to wriggle through with some determination. Yet it was the only answer. Which meant ... the realisation dawned on me that Lady Martha must be out in the field with the entire herd of horses and ponies! It's fair to say I travelled from the barn to the field with some speed.

As I reached the field, I spotted some ponies to my left and there, tucked in next to the fence, was tiny Lady Martha. She was standing quietly, looking very pleased with herself. She couldn't have been out there very long because the scattered herd was starting to show an interest in her and more ponies were beginning to migrate over. There was no way I could get Lady Martha inside before she was completely surrounded. She would have to deal with this on her own. I swallowed and knew it was crucial for me to remain completely calm. Slowly, the ponies came over and sniffed at Lady Martha. It was fascinating to see her two friends, Monsieur Chapeau and Lady Molly, staying fairly close and also calm, while the other ponies produced a range of responses, from gentle curiosity to some rather haughty flicking back of ears, snaking of heads and necks, and general wariness. Each and every newcomer to a herd has to be weighed, measured and a risk assessment made by the herd members. The priority for any herd is safety and survival and the wrong kind of newcomer can compromise that. So even this tiny foal had to go through the process before the herd decided to accept her – or not.

I was weighing up what on earth to do, when Lady Martha again took the lead. She suddenly decided to trot off, which immediately activated the herd energy. Like a ripple through water, the adrenaline rose and the ponies began to follow her. Lady Martha broke into a canter and was soon taking off around the field (about 16 acres) with the entire herd in hot pursuit. I suppose you could describe my response as 'frozen watchfulness'. A mixture of fascination and horror. The moment before a train crash or something like that. To her credit, she was fast, brave and determined. I realised

Opposite page, clockwise from top left:

Monsieur Chapeau nurturing his new protege.

Getting into the Christmas spirit.

We soon became firm friends.

The Herd 99 colts are now conservation grazing for the Molland Estate.

Right: More ponies migrate over to greet Lady.

Below: Lady Martha suddenly takes off.

Bottom: Activating the herd energy.

that she was shouting to the others, 'Here I am, I'm part of this herd!'

As she circled near me once more, I could see she was wondering whether she'd perhaps bitten off a little more than she could chew and I gestured to her to follow me back down the track and into the barn. This she duly did, with her enthusiastic entourage in tow. We zipped in through the doors and I gestured to her to come with me ... quickly ... as I opened the pen door. Lady Martha flew inside and we both stared at each other. She busied herself with her milk – there had been no time to move it and give it back to her when everything had calmed down. She looked immensely pleased with herself. Everyone else thought this was enormous fun and there was much prancing and posturing in the barn before the herd took off outside again.

'Thanks Lady Martha, now do you realise why I'm trying to work out how to socialise you gradually into the herd?' I said to her, assuming that due to the effort that must have been required to wriggle out of the pen, it would be a one off.

Nevertheless, the following day, this was repeated. Tucking Lady Martha comfortably into her pen

Above left: Martha leading a chase.

Above right: Martha with the herd.

Left: Lady Martha whips up a hooley.

with her late night feed, the following morning, she had again managed to wriggle through the pen railings and this time, she was right out across the field, happily grazing with her new friends. Once again though, she followed me in and returned to the pen for her breakfast.

'OK Lady Martha, I get it. We humans can be a bit slow to catch on sometimes. You want to be with the herd.'

'I need to make her a creep gate, so she can get into the pen for her milk or whenever she needs a rest,' said Nick.

What a brilliant idea.

So a short while later, Nick had constructed a gate with a narrow gap that only tiny Lady Martha would be able to pass through. It went into the shute which then opened into her pen area. How on earth were we going to teach this tiny foal to use it though?

There were no worries there. As bright as a button, Lady Martha quickly worked out that when she came in through the stock gate and had her milk, the way out was through the shute and creep gate. When she was hungry again, I brought the milk and squeezed in through the creep gate myself, and she followed me in. The penny dropped and soon Lady Martha was whizzing in and out of her creep gate with glee.

While we thought she'd use the pen to rest and lie down in, she mostly chose to sleep in the larger barn area, often to be found flat out and surrounded by the herd. Her time in the pen was mostly about eating and then returning to the herd as quickly as possible. Lady Martha was offering a wonderful tutorial in the needs and desires of foals for company and to be part of the herd. How miserable and lonely the poor newly weaned foals must be when they're shut away in stables on their own, for weeks and sometimes months on end.

All interactions with Lady Martha had so far been at liberty – from her escape to the pasture, to coming back in again when I asked her, and then learning to use the foal gate. There was clear understanding between us and there had been no need for a head collar and rope. The two-way connection was vibrant and strong. I only had to appear in the barn and Lady Martha would march out from the herd and come with me into the pen. She was quickly learning to read and understand people, and respond appropriately – she was a true survivor. The rest of the herd seemed to understand that the foal needed her milk – later supplemented with foal creep pellets – and required 'special privileges' and there was no barging or crowding to try and get into the pen for her refreshments. Most importantly, with this system young Lady Martha could mature and develop within a sociable herd environment – rather than as an isolated and artificially bottle-reared foal.

Opposite page, clockwise from top left: Lady Molly looks after Lady Martha; Monsieur Chapeau chaperones Lady Martha; surrounded by the herd; Lady Martha sticks close to Monsieur Chapeau.

Top: Lady Martha's foal creep gate.
Above centre: Only Lady Martha could get in and out.
Above: Spending time with the herd in the barn.

Chapter Three
Working with Herds

An increasing number of ponies requires creative thinking and brings new insights

We now had three distinct herds running in three separate areas on the farm – the large herd; stallion Bear and his brood mares; and two other brood mares running with their filly daughters.

As winter stretched towards spring, careful management of ponies and pasture was needed. Part of our management system is ensuring that all the ponies have access to comfortable, covered loafing areas which give them some time off the grass and respite from bad weather. Using good quality, alkaline sea sand in these areas is proving to be successful. It has multiple benefits – being clean, slightly antiseptic and gently exfoliating, the sand deals with the arrival of muddy ponies brilliantly, removing mud and cleaning their feet, legs and coats. They enjoy standing, playing and lying down, it's easy to skip out and every now and again, we cultivate the surfaces, adding fresh sand when necessary. These areas can also double up as excellent surfaces for handling and training.

With a large number of ponies in the main herd, including the now flourishing little Lady Martha, we had to adapt and evolve our handling approach and routine to look after them – and ourselves. The herds have the freedom to migrate in and out as they wish and while calling a couple of horses in from the field is one thing, calling twenty-plus ponies and horses in at the same time is something quite different. Especially if they're keen to see you – or rather, keen to see their fresh haylage. (This is cut grass which is baled and then wrapped in plastic, making it moister and more nutritious than plain hay.) With no staff and a lot of ponies, along with the rest of the farm to run, Nick and I have to think outside of the box regarding their management, care and development – and create a system that suits us and the ponies.

The Haylage Bar
Some careful planning was needed to work out how to best feed forage to the big herd. Ponies can be understandably keen to get to food and there are some lively interactions if they have to jostle to reach piles of haylage. This can result in it being pulled about all over the place, trodden on, soiled and very quickly turned into a mess that requires constant clearing up – and wastage. The pushier ponies can also start guarding piles, stopping more introverted, placid herd members from reaching the food.

Calling in the herd.

Opposite: The Holtball Herd 11 Exmoor ponies.

Lady Martha and her spacehopper.

Lady Martha joining Monsieur Chapeau's social group for haylage.

Right: The herd enjoying their haylage bar.

Something had to be organised where everyone could feed and where the feed mostly reached its target – their stomachs rather than going straight to the muck-heap.

Nick came up with the idea of using tractor tyres as hay feeders. The tyres need to be high enough to discourage the ponies from walking into them, but with the diameter of the hole in the centre large enough so that, in the event one did jump in, there is room to safely and quickly manoeuvre out again easily. The tyres to avoid are those that stand high with a small central space – these can be potentially lethal. After some experimentation, we now have a range of large tyres that do a brilliant job. Spaced a good distance from each other, the ponies can congregate around them, organising

Right: Flanked by protective geldings – Monsieur Chapeau far left.

Far right: Head collar training in the herd's social area.

themselves into their favoured social groups. The rubber exteriors avoid any rubbing or knocks, or tripping, and they can bustle and move around – and also give themselves distance from pushier companions. They reach down into the tyres to eat, working all the right neck muscles – and there is far less wastage than feeding forage on the ground. They can also move quickly if they need to. There can be the odd fracas but these are quickly resolved and the ponies can mostly be found quietly dispersed around the tyres, happily munching hay. Once set up, we referred to this area as 'The Haylage Bar'.

Lady Martha was now part of a happy social group – here with Lady Myrtleberry of Countisbury on the right.

Working her way into the herd

Little Lady Martha liked to move around, eating out of any tyre she fancied and all of the social groups within the herd accepted her nibbling from their tyres, even the dominant veteran Arabian, Casper. Lady Martha appeared keen to ensure that she was fully accepted within the entire herd – giving a good demonstration of how the equine social structure works with regard to integration and survival. Although she had no mother to care for her, she certainly knew how to gain the friendship, or at the very least the tolerance, of the various herd members. She was also working her way through large bags of mare replacement milk and foal creep pellets – at a considerable cost – which could potentially ruffle the feathers of any farmer. However, Lady Martha had an uncanny knack of searching Nick out and looking for a fuss. She was affectionate and endearing and I could see he had a soft spot for her – a very smart foal indeed.

At times, the scale of the resource required for the pony project along with the winter chores could take some facing. But when we found ourselves pushing seemingly endless heavy wheelbarrows late at night, I only had to meet the gaze of Lady Martha, Monsieur Chapeau, or any of the other ponies who wouldn't be here if it wasn't for our project, for a renewed surge of energy that it's all worth the effort.

From top: Lady Martha searches Nick out for a fuss.

A mischievious nature.

Seeking friendship with Firestar (or at least tolerance).

The herd nurturing Lady Martha.

A filming challenge

In the spring we had the opportunity to do some filming that would include Monsieur Chapeau, the big herd and our stallion Bear. As readers of *Wild Stallion Whispering* will know, Bear made a spectacular journey from being an unwanted, multiple hot-branded, touch-resistant moorbred colt foal, to becoming a charismatic multi-champion licensed stallion and winning two consecutive world championships in International Horse Agility (through competing in a year-long global league in 2011 and 2012). One of the aims of this filming opportunity was to capture Bear's trademark liberty jump through the giant blue hoop. However, during the past year, Bear had been running with mares who are now both in foal, and his mind was very much on 'being a stallion' rather than a ridden or agility performance pony. I only had a few weeks to reintroduce him to the agility challenges and re-establish our connection.

Bear polishes up his liberty and agility skills

After setting up some agility exercises in the outdoor corral, including a podium, bridge, cone weave, see-saw and the giant hoop jump, I let Bear explore them at liberty. His first response was to trot off to the perimeter, snorting loudly as he gazed up at the moor and then spotted our herd in the adjacent field, full of young fillies. His attention was on everything but me – and agility was the last thing on his mind. So I waited and watched.

Training for two agility world championships has deeply ingrained in me the importance of not putting personal goals before the ponies wellbeing. Working with a steady stream of wild-born foals has taught me patience and the power of the pause. So what we managed to accomplish during the next few weeks would be at Bear's pace. To achieve a high level of performance, the two of us needed a pure understanding and connection – and it would be his willing cooperation that would get the best results. I knew that Bear wouldn't have forgotten a thing – he just had to want to do it.

Today, however, I was wondering how I could even get his attention. Some minutes passed – and my ego nagged at me to 'get him focused'. I resisted – and waited. Eventually, Bear turned to look at me, studying me intently as I stood on the podium. He slowly and purposefully walked across the corral and climbed up onto it with his front feet. I stepped off and he climbed right onto it. He began to turn and gave me the most wonderful pirouette. I praised him and he gave another one. It was a beautiful moment as we began to re-connect. Starting to walk away from the podium, I gestured for him to follow me, but he didn't. So I continued to walk across the corral and waited once again. He studied me for a long moment, then moved off the podium and came over to me. The connection was strong – I had his complete attention and he'd offered me something special of his own free will – his pirouette. This was a good moment to end the session. Twenty minutes of distraction and waiting – and just a few minutes of effective connection. But in those few minutes, Bear had revealed his ability to focus with a positive attitude and keen understanding. As we left the corral, however, he gave a dramatic spook at the giant blue hoop jump as if he'd never seen it before. It was clear we had some work to do.

Reintroducing Bear to agility and re-establishing our connection.

Building confidence with Bear

Over the next couple of sessions, Bear's desire to connect and engage continued to improve. He navigated the flapping plastic curtain, see-saw, cone weave, figure of eight drums, bridge and podium. He even pushed the giant ball — something that had taken a long time for him to accept. Yet he continued to steer well clear of the hoop jump.

So we went completely back to basics, as if he had never seen it before, taking it one tiny step at a time. Soon he was happily walking through the hoop, with the bottom half resting on the ground, then raised a little, then a little more until it made a proper circle. Then I ask him to trot around and jump it properly on his own. He did this with confidence and enthusiasm and wheeled around to me afterwards, extremely pleased with himself. Once again, Bear had shown me that the way forwards is always with patience, calmness and kindness — and by giving him the time he needed to re-build his confidence in the hoop jump.

Our partnership was enjoying an enhanced freshness and a deepened rapport. Working with the wild-born foals had brought greater softness and consideration to my approach. It was clear that Bear appreciated this and I felt closer than ever to this magnificent stallion.

The canter weave — and why this is one of the very best exercises in horse training

One of Bear's favourite challenges is the weave. This exercise requires balance, flexibility and dexterity. It's also a great way to train for suppleness in ridden work. While this is not a 'practical horsemanship book', there is so much to be gained from learning the weave — and understanding how ponies think and learn — that I wanted to share it. There is a massive difference between 'making a pony go in and out of objects' and developing the flow, harmony and mutual understanding that is possible between pony and handler — when navigating a weave with willing partnership. It's an outstanding exercise in two-way communication and paves the way for working with groups of ponies and herds.

A weave can be created with about six objects — poles, cones, buckets, drums, big logs or basically anything that a pony can safely navigate around. The pony can start off in a head collar and long rope (about 12ft) and progress to doing it at liberty.

The aim is to establish a good connection with the whole of the pony's body, from head to tail, including all four feet. (For more details, pony handlers can reference the Practical Section in *Wild Stallion Whispering* for the Core Connection Warm-Up Exercises.) The idea is to gently and smoothly ask the pony to 'send' away around each weave cone and then 'draw' back through — with the handler directing without touching the pony. There's no need for whips/sticks, pulling on the rope, pushing or shouting.

When the pony is confident going in and out of the cones, the handler can progress to walking down the outside of the cones, while asking the pony to weave in and out himself. When this is well established on the long lead rope, it can be tried at liberty.

Opposite: With patience and calmness Bear regained his confidence with the Giant Hoop Jump.

Core Energy Connection

Ponies are well aware of the energy radiating from our heart and solar plexus areas, down our arms and through our fingertips – tuning into this energy enhances the clarity of our requests. We can both send and receive it, exchanging information and intention and establishing two-way communication. People who aren't aware of their own core energy (who are 'flat' and detached in the mid-section of the body) have to work harder, because they are just giving directions without 'feel' – a bit like trying to sing on a stage without a microphone.

The handler ideally stays in the shoulder area of the pony, with their arm and hand working to guide the pony. They can pick up an 'energy connection' with the pony, drawing their outer arm and hand towards their body to draw the pony towards them, and then radiating it outwards to 'send' him away again – as they progress in and out of the cones. Taking care not to 'block' the connection by turning their back on the pony as they move together.

Once the weave is going well at a walk, it can be done at a trot. Starting at a slow jog, the handler needs to stay calm. This is not about 'pushing' the pony through the weave, it's about gently guiding – taking care to keep the adrenaline down, and only raising the appropriate energy to increase the pace.

Ponies can get excited when there is an increase in pace, especially when working at liberty. This is usually the result of an adrenaline surge and slight anxiety/excitement about what they're doing – and what their handler is doing. It can be alarming for ponies when people get excitable when they're in close proximity and it takes some practice to raise energy (ie break into a run) but not let your adrenaline shoot up alongside. That makes us 'unpredictable' to a pony who may respond with inappropriate behaviour like a kick or bite. So it's essential to remain calm and clear in making requests, taking care not to drop behind the shoulder and into the kick zone. Once the weave is completed, the handler can ask the pony to move his quarters away and draw his head around for a safe finish.

It can take some time to perfect the weave at trot, and canter should only really be attempted when the pony is well balanced and confident at trot. A canter weave can be started using just three cones spaced well apart. We're looking for a smooth walk to canter transition, with a raise in energy, but not adrenaline. Again, it's not about 'making' the pony canter, it's asking for a canter transition – and there's a big difference.

The handler's body language needs to be smooth, clear and quick – which is why practising the drawing and sending signals with the guiding hand working from the mid area of the body is effective. There's no time for arm waving or any erratic gestures. It's a smooth flow of fingertip signals saying, 'Go' and 'Come' – with the handler's body angled correctly so as not to block the pony, so he can read it and respond.

Mastering the canter weave provides an all-round skill set for pony and handler.

The canter weave can be tried at the end of a training session where afterwards, the reward is to end the session and relax. Once the three cones are mastered, more cones can be added over further sessions. The aim is to achieve a balanced canter down the cones, with the pony sitting back on his hocks, lifting himself in front and producing natural flying changes as he adjusts his weight to navigate the cones. For ridden horses and ponies, this translates beautifully into improved balance, lightness, impulsion and suppleness. Importantly, this exercise develops mutual trust as the pony allows the handler to run next to him, with raised energy – safely.

Where mastering the weave can take you

Once the weave is nailed, both pony and handler have the skill set for attempting just about any agility challenge, as well as improving riding, driving, jumping, showing in hand and general leading. Above all there is enhanced mutual trust, understanding and connection. I've found this exercise invaluable for evolving communication with more than one pony and ultimately – when I'm working with herds. It's a great way to get yourself understood by ponies – nicely – and for them to express themselves to us.

Developing connection with the whole herd

While Bear was progressing well, I also had to prepare the big herd for filming. The ponies had to be comfortable with strangers walking among them carrying some unusual equipment. If unsure, they would likely remain wary and maintain what they considered a safe distance from any potential 'risk'. They also needed to come to the call.

I always try to ensure there's something interesting and pleasurable for the ponies as a consequence of them taking notice of me and doing when I ask. This can be something simple like providing some fresh haylage and to interact with and groom them. It's not unreasonable for them to ask, 'What's in it for us?'

I also use different 'energies' to communicate my intention. So, for example, if I walk quietly into the field and mingle with the herd, greeting, stroking and brushing them – they'll interact but realise

The herd in the pasture.

Connecting and bonding with the herd outside and inside.

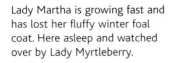

Lady Martha is growing fast and has lost her fluffy winter foal coat. Here asleep and watched over by Lady Myrtleberry.

that I don't necessarily want them to come in. I can then walk away again and leave them to continue grazing. However, when I walk out to the field and stand there with a feeling of energy, intention and add a call, the sentry ponies (the ones assigned to look out and, if necessary, instigate movement) become alert and the herd starts migrating over to me – and usually comes in. It sounds obvious, but calling to a large herd in a 'flat' and unconnected way can easily result in being ignored – particularly if the area is large and most of the ponies are out of sight. There's also a difference between 'herding' ponies in and 'drawing' them in. In the run up to doing the filming, I practised connecting with the ponies and moving them to and from different areas – as a herd. Sometimes, I got to sit amongst them when they were lying down. They were interested and engaging and, hopefully, they would prove to be the same on the day.

Ponies on film

Filming day arrived and after going out to the fields and grooming the ponies, Bear was first on the list. He was calm, poised and focused – performing some lovely pirouettes, weaves and hoop jumps. He stood quietly and patiently while we talked and presented his best behaviour. This cooperation required particular patience on his part as one of his mares was very shortly due to foal, which can cause stallions to become distracted. Afterwards, I returned a grateful Bear to his mares.

Following a quick lunch, the big herd were next on the list. Monsieur Chapeau and Lady Stumpkin Pumpkin were waiting expectantly at the gate with a distinct air of anticipation – they clearly knew they'd been brushed for a reason. As we walked amongst them, the ponies were calm, inquisitive and accepting of the camera crew. They followed us across the field and there were some lovely interactions. The next task was to take the herd to another field, where they would be filmed cantering down a steep

Relaxed and curious the ponies allowed the cameras near.

Dawn and Bear.

slope to the stream and their mud wallow area — and the director asked me how on earth I was going to achieve that. For a moment, I wondered that myself. Just feel it, I thought, and it will happen. Believe in the connection with the herd. Left with the ponies, while the cameras got in position, I focused on the energy radiating from my solar plexus area and conveyed my intention that we needed to move — all together. There was a tangible feeling of connection and they started to lift their heads from the grass and give me their attention. Something was about to happen and they were interested. We started to migrate across the field. There are different characters in the herd — some who are alert and respond immediately, others who take their lead from the leaders, then some who are more introverted and cautious but who pick up on the fact something's happening and come along — and a few who stay at

Bear is engaged and interested for the filming.

the back and eventually come along because they don't want to be left behind. Once the ponies realised we were heading towards the gate which led down to the stream and mud wallow, a ripple of excitement radiated through them, and they gathered enthusiastically behind me. The camera crew were then treated to the wonderful sight of them flowing down the hill to the stream, where they whirled around, leaping and prancing. Monsieur Chapeau took a starring role by lying down and rolling right in front of us.

I couldn't have asked for more and we then headed off to the moor to complete the filming with some free-livings ponies. A successful day, some useful footage – and an enhanced connection with our entire herd.

Dawn with the ponies during filming.

Above left: Monsieur Chapeau offering a fantastic roll at the wallow.

Above right and right: The herd offer some wonderful interactions.

Nick and Dawn Westcott with Monsieur Chapeau.

Why ponies love to get down and dirty

Exmoor ponies love to play in muddy wallows – in both summer and in freezing winter. On a cold, wet and windy day, this can be hard to understand. But sudden bursts of cold on the skin (like cold showers) increase heat producing brown fat cells. The mud, when dried off, acts as a fantastic protection – against the cold in winter, and against flies and midges in summer. Ponies who utilise the mud like this usually have the fluffiest, shiniest, healthiest coats when cleaned off again. A coat in good condition has strong hair, leaving a healthy shine when the mud falls off – or when it's removed through mutual grooming. Wallowing and grooming is a huge part of herd life and being free to move around the pasture and loafing areas, after a mud bath, enables the ponies to maximise their circulation and keep warm. It's amazing how ponies can look like hippos one minute and be shiny and fluffy again not long afterwards. Once again, the herd is showing us what ponies ideally want in the way of healthy living – given the choice.

Monty after a mud wallow session!

This is a somewhat of a contrast to clipped out, rugged-up ponies, standing for long hours in small stables, who are denied this natural social herd activity and the opportunity to regulate their own coats as they want and need to. In the past, I'd thought these pampered and squeaky clean ponies were the lucky ones, but now I'm not so sure – and realising that ponies might well ask for a different, freer and altogether grubbier kind of lifestyle, if given the opportunity.

The ponies use the wallowing areas all year round – both to insulate against cold and protect themselves from flies and midges.

Chapter Four

Foals & Youngsters

Out on the moor and at home there are some special new arrivals

From the wilds of Buscombe – a moorland enclosure adjacent to Brendon Common in Exmoor National Park – there came the news that some new foals had been spotted in the Farleywater herd. This was exciting for us, because some of these spring arrivals would be stallion Bear's first ever foals born into a free-living herd. Buscombe comprises several hundred acres of challenging, boggy, dramatic terrain in the heart of Exmoor, so the foals get a wonderful start in life traversing the moorland sedge grasses and living wild and free. We very much hoped that one particular mare, Foxglove, would produce a colt foal who might show stallion potential.

Bear had covered a small group of the semi-feral Farleywater mares the previous year, who had then returned to Buscombe where another stallion, Wortleberry, was running with the rest of the herd. Living in such a remote area, the mares can be shy of visitors, so we'd probably have to wait until the autumn gatherings to find out for sure which mares had produced which foals.

After Bear had returned home, he'd run with our own mares, Penelope Pitstop and Maisie, so we were also expecting two Herd 11 foals this year.

Bear's first wild-born foals out on Buscombe.

Opposite page: Holtball Kick-em Jenny with her daughter Holtball Princess Cristal and Anstey Princess with her daughter Holtball Black Bess – and Monty in the background.

Anstey Princess with her daughter Holtball Black Bess, and Holtball Kick-em Jenny with her daughter Princess Cristal.

Merging herds brings a whole new dynamic

Our homebred yearling fillies Holtball Princess Cristal and Black Bess had remained with their mothers, Jenny and Anstey Princess, in a separate little herd during the past year. There was no pressing need to wean 'Bessie' and 'Cristal', but they could ideally do with some more playmates. Introducing them into the big herd would assist with natural weaning and enable them to meet new friends with their mothers alongside.

First of all, gelding Monty joined their group. He had sired Princess Cristal before being gelded as a five year old and it was lovely for him to be able to meet his daughter. While Jenny was very pleased to see Monty, Anstey Princess was certainly not and displayed some magnificent body language.

But she soon calmed down and the fillies showed great interest in both Monty and then Monsieur Chapeau, when he also joined the group. It was all progressing well and I was thinking about starting the introductions to the main herd when, once again, the ponies took matters into their own hands.

That evening, when I went out to check the mares and fillies in the twilight, I could see that a significant number of extra ponies had managed to get in with them. As I peered out into their pasture, some sudden squealing revealed their whereabouts. I called softly to Anstey Princess and Jenny and they and their daughters started to trot towards me — displaying that amazing connection ponies have when they realise it is specifically them you want, out of a larger group. I gestured to them to quickly follow me into the corral and through into the barn, giving me just enough time to shut the doors so the enthusiastic band of ponies who were now following them could not get in as well. We all looked at each other rather wide-eyed. Checking them over, they were all fine, and I was soon able to re-organise everyone back into the right enclosures.

While Jenny is happy to see Monty, Anstey Princess is not.

Merging the herds together.

The next day, I let a small group from the main herd in with the mares and yearlings, which included youngsters Lady Martha, Lady Molly, Lady Myrtleberry and Jenny's two year old daughter Princess Khaleesi. This gave them the opportunity to make some more introductions before letting the full herd run together. Monty and Monsieur Chapeau proved to be good mediators and chaperones. While the two older mares were aloof and protective, the young fillies were keen to make new friends.

After opening up all of their pasture areas and finally allowing both herds to properly mingle with plenty of space, the brood mares protected their daughters robustly, yet allowed them to greet and explore the other ponies. Our older gelding Harry took on the role of a chivalrous and protective 'stallion' – first challenging Monty and then following Jenny and Anstey Princess and their daughters around, guarding them, lying down next to them – and not leaving them for an instant, day or night. If we were anthropomorphising, I might say he'd fallen head over heels in love!

Monsieur Chapeau meeting Black Bess.

The challenges of being a two year old

Soon an equilibrium within the now larger herd had been reached and Cristal and Bessie were gaining some much needed socialisation and making new friends. It was also an opportunity for Jenny's other daughter, two year old Princess Khaleesi, to be re-aquainted with her mother – and to get to know her new sister Cristal. However, it took a period of time for Jenny to allow Khaleesi near and it couldn't have been easy for the two year old to watch her once devoted mother nurturing another daughter – while pushing her away.

It's common for two-year-old equines to experience a loss of status – a kind of 'no-mans land' –

Above, left to right: Lady Martha meeting Cristal with Jenny allowing the interaction;
Jenny watches closely as Black Bess and Cristal greet Lady Martha;
Two-year-old Khaleesi (second from left) is rebuffed by her own mother while Cristal is showing submission to her.

Right and below: Harry challenging Monty for Jenny and Cristal.

Harry (third from left) guarding Jenny and Cristal from Blossom.

between being the centre of attention as a foal and becoming a mature herd member. In free-living herds, it is the two year olds who are 'expendable'. They are required to stand on their own four feet and look out for themselves, yet are not old enough to breed. Once they make it to three or four years old, their importance within the herd increases and they in turn look down their noses at the upcoming two year olds. I suppose it can be considered a 'right of passage' into the adult herd.

Two year old Princess Khaleesi had to be patient to be accepted by her mother once again.

Everything soon settled down in the herd.

Penelope Pitstop and her new son Pierre Parfait.

Penelope Pitstop extends us an enormous privilege

Spring brought the arrival of Penelope Pitstop's very first foal. Usually, the mares are secretive and despite checking them in the early hours and first thing in the morning, they will inevitably produce their foals when no-one is around, overseen by the now very experienced Bear. However, Penelope proved to be different. Checking on her late one evening, I found her sedately lying down in the barn. After we'd skipped out, Nick started walking back to the house and as I turned to go, Penelope got up. I stood watching her as she circled around and then lay down and got up again. Suddenly, there was a whooshing sound and her waters broke.

Nick came back and as we watched, Penelope approached me and touched my hand and began slowly walking around. We could see the bubble of the birth sack emerging.

'Oh my goodness, she's going to foal now, right in front of us,' I said in amazement.

We stood quietly, just outside of the enclosure, not interfering unless we were needed. It didn't take long and very soon afterwards, Penelope was licking at a beautiful little colt foal. She had wanted to foal with us there and made it very clear that we were welcome. I gently approached and Penelope introduced me to her new son. Checking that everything looked alright, we left them in peace for a few hours, watched over by Bear and Maisie.

No to imprinting

Unless there is a veterinary need, we prefer not to interfere in the early mare/foal bond and do no invasive handling. I'm not a fan of 'imprinting' where the newborn foal is extensively handled to prepare for human contact. We prefer foals to know they are ponies first and foremost. From there a willing connection with humans can build, which is very much on the foal's terms and is developed at liberty. I believe this helps to create ponies who are ultimately able to form more confident and trusting relationships with people over the longer term. Foals can 'internalise' experiences they dislike – or which frighten, overwhelm them or cause them pain – and these feelings can manifest themselves later on with undesirable and unpredictable behaviours and responses.

'What shall we call him?' I pondered and took the question to our social media. Penelope Pitstop had acquired her name when the 'Wacky Races' programme had been the theme for her breeder. A popular suggestion was Peter Perfect but there was already a pony of that name in the stud book. It was Josephine who came up with the great idea of taking a French theme. We already had Monsieur Chapeau so what better to call the new foal than Pierre Parfait? Once suggested, the name stuck.

A few weeks later, Pierre Parfait was zipping around, and perhaps a little too enthusiastically, because I noticed his previously perfect baby teeth were missing a front tooth – he'd knocked it out somewhere. Fortunately, he seemed comfortable enough and hopefully everything will even up when his second teeth eventually come through. We didn't want Bear to cover Penelope again so she and Pierre Parfait moved to a different field soon after he was born and before Penelope's foal heat. It was a shame that Bear didn't get to spend more time with his son but we, along with other breeders, have had to exercise restraint over our breeding programmes in a tough market for ponies.

Pierre Parfait proves to be quite a character!

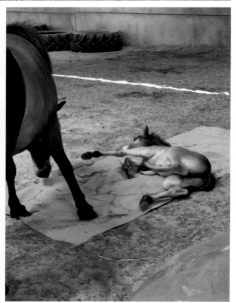

Pierre Parfait gets himself in trouble

Pierre Parfait was certainly proving to be quite a character. One day when I checked the ponies, to my horror I found Pierre Parfait standing with his head lowered and thick globules of greeny saliva drooling out of his nose and mouth. He was subdued and rather stressed.

'Oh my God Pierre, have you bitten a toad?' I remembered seeing the very same response from our Jack Russell, Minot, having found him after a battle with a toad. It had taken much washing and a good drink of diluted milk to sort him out. But I didn't think it would be usual for a foal to go around biting toads – and then I realised he was choking. The vet was called immediately.

When he arrived, poor Pierre Parfait was lying down in the barn being stroked by me and anxiously watched over by Penelope. She had realised he needed help and was very accommodating. Pierre let me slip on a head collar and as Nick went to embrace him in a gentle hug so the vet could examine him, he gave a lurch and launched back towards Nick, landing with a thump on the sandy bed.

'Oh, is he OK?' I said. As we watched him, he started looking more alert. The vet examined him and over the next few minutes, it was clear that Pierre Parfait was starting to feel better. It seemed that the thump on the ground must have dislodged whatever it was. He was a very lucky boy. I wouldn't recommend this as a course of treatment for a choking foal, but it certainly worked for Pierre Parfait!

Pierre Parfait proved to be playful, mischievous and endearing. He and Penelope Pitstop grazed in a home paddock where they also had access to the barn and agility objects at times. This gave Pierre the opportunity to explore exciting new things and play with them. They were also next to a field into which the big herd migrated from time to time. I would often find them both up at the fence, grazing as close as they could to the other ponies – Penelope staring wistfully at the herd, with Pierre either zooming about or, very often, fast asleep in the grass. He was still very small, but I began to wonder – thinking of Lady Martha – whether it would be possible to introduce them into the big herd at some point soon. Penelope knew a lot of the ponies very well – and she had lived with some of them since she'd arrived as a newly weaned foal from the moor.

If it hadn't been for Lady Martha's astonishing escape into the herd at only about six weeks old, I would never have considered it, fearing for Pierre's safety amongst such a large group. But the herd had educated us that far more was possible than we had imagined.

Opposite page:

Top right: Pierre Parfait spends a great deal of time sleeping, watched over by Penelope.

Top left: Mischievous Pierre Parfait discovers the teleporter bucket.

Centre left: Playing with the spacehopper.

Bottom centre: Sniffing noses with Monsieur Chapeau through the gate.

Bottom right: Discovering the tarpaulin.

Chapter Five

Freedom, Movement & Herd Connection

A spacious environment for the herd brings new understanding and friendships

By summer, the home paddocks needed a good rest, some maintenance and cross-grazing by the sheep – and the herd needed some fresh ground and new experiences. Nick suggested a group of fields further down the farm, which he felt would provide an excellent environment for them. The grass in one field had been let up and was to be managed through grazing, rather than cutting for hay. It had already seeded in the dry, hot weather and was tall and bleached, with the new sward starting to grow underneath. The adjoining field had just been cut for haylage and was short and bleached with very little sward. The third field had been grazed tight by sheep. This field is fascinating and comprises an area of dramatic humps, rather like a dome. Animals love grazing up there in the hot summer months because the peculiar vortexes created by the wind keep midges away, making it cool and refreshing.

'Won't there be too much grass?' I asked concerned, as some horse owners are now putting their equines onto track systems with little or no grass.

'I don't think so,' said Nick. He felt there was a good range of options for the ponies with no areas of lush, rich grass – and a layout that lent itself to migrating around.

'When they eat this long, dried grass, they'll get a good amount of roughage, along with a bit of the newer sward,' he said.

The big herd exploring their spacious new summer environment.

Anstey Princess and Black Bess remained together in the big herd.

Groups of youngsters tended to band together – Monsieur Chapeau here with Topaz and Princess Khaleesi.

The approximately 30 acre enclosure, along with the slopes and domed areas, offered a wonderful environment for the herd. There was no barn shelter here, but it was bounded by thick tree-lined hedges offering plenty of natural shelter. It certainly looked exciting. But not as exciting for me as it did to the herd. When they saw me open the field gate and call to them, the more extrovert ponies immediately started to canter down towards me, soon followed by all the others. They flowed across the lane and into the new fields and off they went, exploring the new area with gregarious joy. After galloping large circles, they dropped their heads to graze.

As Nick had predicted, the herd soon migrated to the top of the humpy field, where it was breezy and refreshing. One of the mares, Blossom, who suffers from sweet itch, found the absence of midges and flies a great relief and she ended up spending a large amount of her time at the top of the humps.

Penelope Pitstop and Pierre Parfait watched them longingly from their paddock above the lane. They were now alone.

Groups within groups – insights into the herd's social structure

In this new and spacious environment, the various social groups within the herd became more apparent. The two mares, Jenny and Anstey Princess remained together with their yearling daughters, chaperoned by the geldings, Harry and Monty. Monty also spent a lot of time with his two year old daughter Princess Khaleesi. It had been a difficult decision to geld such a beautiful little stallion, but seeing him enjoying an interesting and sociable life in the herd was reassuring. The lot of a stallion can be quite lonely and frustrating at times. Some mature stallions accept the company of other males, but not all, especially when there are mares and fillies in the vicinity. Monty now enjoyed all the benefits of life in a large herd.

There is a distinct group of the Farleywater ponies, which also includes Imperial Topaz who joined them as a newly weaned foal in 2013. The Holtball Herd 11 youngstock tend to migrate around together, while the Molland Moor ponies and Monsieur Chapeau and Lady Myrtleberry of Countisbury mingle and mix.

The Farleywater fillies, Pumpkin, Scarlet and Firestar remain a close group, here with Lady Martha.

Monty and his daughter Princess Khaleesi.

The herd love to graze on top of the humps where it is cool and breezy watched over here by Jimbo the sheepdog.

Opposite: Calling the herd back up to the farm.

When horses and ponies are able to socialise naturally in a herd environment, with a degree of freedom, they display a wide range of emotions and behaviours. They are lively, passionate and expressive – and an incredible, tangible sense of herd energy develops. They form close bonds, spending time playing, resting and grooming with favoured companions. They have their likes and dislikes, which can include outbursts of annoyance, jealousy and even tantrums. There is a continual testing of status within the herd and challenges to the hierarchy, with ponies looking to assert, dominate – or submit – in myriad situations and ways, on many levels – every day. The herd social structure is elastic, flexible and ever-evolving.

The herd members watch and take in everything going on around them, for as far as their eyes can see – and beyond through their amazing hearing. Whatever they are doing at any particular time, and no matter how widely they're dotted about in various of the fields – in sight or out of sight of each other – they all remain strongly connected as a herd, ready to re-group and move together in an instant, if the need arises.

Little Lady Martha of Molland Moor was by now well established in the big herd. She had been taken into the fold and nurtured beautifully. She had firm friends in Monsieur Chapeau, Lady Molly and Lady Myrtleberry. However, one of the most touching and endearing friendships of all was about to begin.

Big herd recall

From time to time, we would have to bring the herd back up to the farm for management, training and handling. It was one thing turning them all out into the large area of pasture away from the farm, but some thought had to go into how to bring them all back home again. With three large fields spanning some 40 or so acres, it could well turn out to be like herding cats.

It transpired that the herd remained highly responsive – even at a considerable distance. I was able to call to them from across the fields, where they were literally dots on the horizon, often grazing on top of their beloved humps. The sentry ponies spotted us, took a few moments to assess the situation and then they started to stream down from the humps and disappear into the dips, drawing the other ponies with them. Appearing again over the brow of the hill, they cantered across the final field towards us. It was quite emotional to experience the power and beauty of the herd as both the Exmoor ponies and Arabian horses thundered across the pasture and flowed up into the home paddocks. Even the stragglers caught up quickly. The herd was enthusiastic and responsive, whether being asked to return to their summer pastures, or come back up to the farm. They had amazing recall and later on in the year, this was something we would be very grateful for.

Preparing Penelope Pitstop and Pierre Parfait for some new company

Over in their home paddock, it was clear that Penelope Pitstop and her son Pierre Parfait could benefit from some company. Pierre Parfait needed some playmates and Penelope was having as much fun as any single mother spending 24/7 alone with her child. Everyone needs a break sometimes.

Right: Bringing groups of ponies back up to the farm sometimes, for handling and training sessions, including agility.

Top: Pierre Parfait is ready for some new friends and playtime!

Centre: Monsieur Chapeau greets Penelope and Pierre.

Bottom: Pierre Parfait makes the foal gesture of submission by snapping his jaws together.

Foals and youngstock need to be able to run about a lot, ideally including on some sloping ground, playing and play-fighting, developing their joints and bones and finding their balance and locomotion. Physically and mentally, it's great for their development and it's why the free-living foals out on the moor get such a wonderful start in life. Our own mares can't currently run out on the adjacent moorland, without risk of getting in foal to stallions or unlicensed entire colts from other herds. So we've had to create the best environment we can, in ground on the farm.

To prepare Penelope Pitstop and Pierre Parfait for integration into the main herd, I brought a small group of ponies back up to the farm to introduce into their paddock. While Penelope had grown up with most of the older members of the herd, there were plenty of our young project ponies that she hadn't been turned out with. I wanted to ensure that some carefully monitored introductions were made before she and Pierre Parfait joined the large herd.

Pierre Parfait meets Monsieur Chapeau

Monsieur Chapeau was the first to be introduced, initially greeting them over the fence and gate. Penelope was protective and dramatic and Monsieur Chapeau remained very calm, well used to exuberant mares. He was fascinated by the little foal and the feeling was mutual. As Penelope became more

Penelope Pitstop and Pierre Parfait meet the whole herd.

accepting, I let Monsieur Chapeau into the paddock with them. From her demeanour, it appeared that Penelope actually quite liked him and he was on his very best behaviour. Pierre approached him making the submissive foal mouthing gesture and Penelope looked on quietly – allowing the interaction. It was a special moment. Shortly afterwards, I introduced a few other ponies and once these introductions were made and the small group were happily grazing together, it was time for the next stage.

Penelope and Pierre Parfait join the big herd
If we turned Penelope and Pierre Parfait out into the fields with the big herd, they would be conspicuous as 'newcomers' (even though a good number already knew Penelope) and liable to be chased around. So instead, I called the herd up into the home paddocks to meet them. The ponies and horses migrated up into the large field where Penelope, Pierre Parfait and their companions were grazing. There was plenty of space and Pierre Parfait stuck close to his mother as she greeted the ponies and made it very clear that she would protect her foal. Introductions were made and Penelope quickly re-connected with her long-standing companions, while asserting to the younger new acquaintances that she was not going to be anywhere near the bottom of the pecking order. Pierre Parfait tentatively sniffed noses and appeared curious rather than nervous. Shortly afterwards, the herd returned to their summer grazing fields, this time joined by Penelope Pitstop and Pierre Parfait who were clearly delighted to be amongst all the ponies they had watched longingly from the isolation of their own paddock.

Introducing Penelope and Pierre Parfait to a smaller group of ponies first.

A special friendship begins

Lady Martha found Pierre Parfait and Penelope Pitstop almost immediately. She was absolutely entranced by a foal smaller than herself, who was still with his mother, and it may well have stirred feelings for the mother she had been separated from at such a young age. While Penelope was forthright in rebuffing the prospect of a second older foal to look after, Pierre was captivated with Lady Martha.

Penelope soon established that, a) she was now part of the big herd so they'd better all get used to it, b) Pierre Parfait was her foal, and c) Lady Martha was not her foal. After the initial excitement had calmed down, Lady Martha followed Penelope and Pierre Parfait everywhere, with Penelope periodically pushing and even chasing her off when she got too close. However, Lady Martha's determination to join the small herd of mare and foal was greater than Penelope's determination to push her away and soon, she and Pierre Parfait were a small herd of three, although Penelope would not permit Lady Martha to suckle. The two youngsters played happily together and Pierre Parfait's world had now expanded enormously, with life in the big herd providing an amazing environment for him. Interestingly, once settled, Penelope was happy for Martha and Pierre to wander off together, sometimes to an adjoining field, while she grazed. It seemed that within the safety of a large herd, she felt it acceptable to let her foal play at a distance, for some of the time at least. Lady Martha behaved very much like a big sister to Pierre – protective, bustling and attentive. She clearly adored him. Suddenly, she was no longer the baby of the herd and it gave her a new sense of self importance and purpose.

Below and centre: Lady Martha and Pierre Parfait adore each other.

Below right: Pierre Parfait is inquisitive and cheeky.

Above: Pierre Parfait wants to play with Lady Martha.

Far left: Always together.

Left: Pierre Parfait and his mother Penelope grooming.

Maintaining connection with the big herd at pasture

While the ponies were thoroughly enjoying their spacious new environment, I also needed to continue their handling and training. When Exmoor ponies – particularly those who are wild-born – are left to their own devices, they can sometimes revert towards a 'semi-feral' state. Especially those with a naturally more wary disposition.

Leaving youngsters unhandled for significant periods can make ongoing socialisation tricky as they get bigger and stronger – and more independent thinking. I had quite a job on my hands working out how to maintain a degree of individual connection with so many ponies. A small and distinct group of them tended to remain more elusive, hovering behind the others. They were receptive to recall and interested in connecting, but hesitant to come right up close and be stroked or have a head collar on. This group included three year old Tom Faggus and our own homebred two year old Prince Kailash. Soon, these ponies would need to come back up to the farm for some day to day contact and handling.

Whenever possible, I spent time in the pasture with the herd, wandering amongst them and interacting, grooming and giving them individual attention. Sometimes, I was accompanied by a

While dramatic gestures are often what we focus on, the subtle behaviours reveal so much about how ponies communicate.

friend. The herd would inevitably be spread out in their social 'sub-groups' and meandering around and engaging with them preserved a sentient connection – rather like keeping in touch with friends and family. Most of the time though, I was alone with the herd and this gave me the opportunity to tune into their energy and dynamics. Sometimes, I'd find them relaxing and they'd let me join them to sit or lie down with them – accepting me into their midst. As Winston Churchill said, 'There is something about the outside of a horse that's good for the inside of a man,' and he was so right. It's not possible to spend time with the herd without coming away feeling refreshed, energised and inspired. Happy horses and ponies radiate positive, powerful energy and I continued to learn about their need for space, environment and a sociable herd life.

Seeing beyond the dramatic – a world of communication awaits us

In the modern world, there is much focus on the more dramatic – and even aggressive – interactions between horses. Rearing, leaping, fighting postures and *airs above the ground*, galloping about – these are all familiar sights on TV when horses are involved. Yet it's the myriad gentle and subtle ways that

Being accepted to relax with the herd is a privilege.

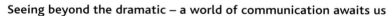

horses maintain a cohesive herd structure, building bonds and friendships – even tolerances – that is fascinating. A herd at pasture offers endless opportunities to observe their communications and through these nuances and interactions, to become better at recognising what they mean, what they're trying to tell us – and to notice when they ask a question or would like attention.

The historic need to train horses for war and work has often meant there was no time or resource to really consider them as sentient individuals, allow them to express their feelings or appreciate their need to maintain herd life and a free-roaming existence. It was all about containment, convenience and obedience. Horses were there to do a job and survival often depended on them doing it well. But now, horses are mostly leisure animals and we have the luxury of being able to listen to them and open our hearts and minds to what they want – and ideally need. By learning more about their sociable interactions – rather than focussing on the small segment of their behaviour when they display angry, aggressive or defensive communications – an entire language emerges that can enhance understanding between horse and human. A tiny tilt, shake or sway of the head, adjustment of expression in the eyes, wrinkling of the brow, flickering of the ears, bracing of the poll or neck, pausing or tensing, or quickening or holding of the breath – which may previously have been missed in the rush to 'catch, groom and ride' – now opens up a world of potential communication and understanding. It's fascinating, for example, to watch a dominant mare literally 'holding' other herd

Watching the subtle gestures, expressions, connections and behaviours is fascinating – up close or at a distance.

Top: Anstey Princess 'holding' Lady Molly back with the swivel and placing of her nearside ear.

Left: Monsieur Chapeau and the herd.

So much passes between ponies through subtle communications.

members in position slightly behind her, by the small movement and placing of an ear. Or influencing the behaviour of a pony at a significant distance in front of her, by a subtle lowering of her head and turning her ears back and slightly outwards. The message conveyed is as clear as day, and read, understood and responded to by the recipient. The language of horses is all around us – and can be easily missed if we are not focussed and in the present moment.

Using energy as a language of communication

Horses and ponies can radiate and read 'energy' – just think of the way they suddenly activate their powerful muscle mass and move in unison, with barely a sound. If we become 'energy aware' as humans, we can also exchange communications with ponies that way. I think of it as 'magnifying' communications. It's rather like turning on a torch beam when we activate our energy centres (particularly the heart and solar plexus areas) – and it's like looking through binoculars to vastly enhance the clarity and focus of what we're seeing.

Through the requirement of dealing with the sheer number of ponies running in a large space, I found communicating with 'energy awareness' invaluable in both managing the herd and maintaining and building relationships with the ponies. It really works. I can connect and exchange information with ponies at a considerable distance and read and understand them better at close quarters. The range and depth of their communications and the way they express themselves – and respond – is amazing and enlightening.

Seeing what is actually there

I'm learning to see what is actually there, rather than what my brain decides it wants me to see. We humans can be inventive and fanciful – and alarmingly assumptive – inside our own heads, without realising it. It takes self-discipline, quietening of ego and spending much time with 'authentic' animals, to develop true observational skills – and horses are some of our greatest teachers.

Some ponies seek a physical greeting and connection; others want acknowledgment and to connect at a distance; some like hands-on grooming, while others remain more aloof. Their moods vary as do their feelings towards each other – and me. Ponies who need something will usually seek me out, particularly if something needs physically tending to. Without fail, little Lady Martha, mostly with Pierre Parfait in tow, always comes up to say hello. Rather than simply 'going to see ponies in the field', it is evolving into me becoming part of their herd energies and dynamics – which is both a privilege and an education. So despite the ponies living at some distance from the actual farm, rather than losing contact with them, my relationship with them is enriching and evolving. They are allowing me into their world, to better understand them.

Pierre Parfait has integrated well into the big herd – here with June.

Chapter Six

Wonderful Walks

What happens when you let go? Building rapport with the ponies on liberty and adventure walks

Exmoor ponies love going out for walks so, when it can be arranged, we take two or three ponies out around the National Trust Holnicote Estate farm fields, the lanes and in the woods and moorland of the adjacent Dunkery Commons.

It's magical when this can be done at liberty – unclipping their lead ropes and letting them come along at their own pace. Of course, on the lanes, it's essential to lead ponies safely on a lead rope, but once on our own farm land, or in the woodland and moorland areas where free-living ponies, cattle, sheep and red deer roam, it's sometimes possible to turn them loose.

Monty is great fun to take out. He's been lightly backed to saddle and also competed successfully in horse agility as a youngster. His recall on the walks is excellent and he sets a great example to the younger ponies coming out to learn the ropes. Monsieur Chapeau also enormously enjoys the walks and if I appear with a head collar, he, Monty and Imperial Topaz are usually the first to come forwards – hoping it's their turn to go out. Closely followed by Lady Stumpkin Pumpkin and Lady Molly.

When walking through the farm fields, we'll often pause for a while and let the ponies explore and graze. In the forest, although the tracks and woodland areas are part of a large moorland area, the ponies stay connected with us. If they get distracted exploring or grazing, they'll soon trot or canter

Opposite: Monsieur Chapeau and Imperial Topaz love their liberty walks.

Below left: Monsieur Chapeau and Topaz lead a liberty walk with Kate and Ollie.

Below right: Sue and June relaxing with the ponies on a walk.

From top:

Monsieur Chapeau is often accompanied by Jimbo the sheep dog;

Monty on a farm liberty walk;

Monsieur Chapeau.

to catch up. It's a wonderful feeling to let them go and know they want to ultimately come along with us. I've learned that the best way to maintain a strong connection is not to 'nag' them. To have the confidence to know that they will re-connect even if there's some distance between us. Together, we are a small herd. Any apprehension or mistrust on my part compromises the connection. The ponies are teaching me to trust them and make that leap of faith to let go – to believe in herd connection, and through that, our mutual bond strengthens. This is being achieved by giving the ponies space, responsibility and freedom – and not trying to 'micro-manage' their every move.

The fear of letting go – and the rewards of doing so

It's clear from how the ponies behave on the liberty walks how much they love being given their freedom – but only when they're confident in their new surroundings. Ponies new to the walks seem to be more comfortable at first being led along on a rope – perhaps it's reassuring for them. Once they understand that going out for walks is safe, and that they always return to their herd, they start to appreciate being let loose.

I hadn't realised how much I'd relaxed on the liberty walks until I took other people along. At first, newcomers could be apprehensive and even mildly anxious.

'Are you really going to turn them loose?'

"How big is this area?'

'What happens if they run off?'

Then some pale faces when I explain that the area is about 5000 acres of moorland and woodland 'wilderness', inhabited by free-living Exmoor ponies, cattle, sheep, red deer and other wildlife...

When we unclip the lead ropes, the new handlers tend to stay close to their pony's side, telling them to, 'Come on, come along,' if the ponies pause even for a moment. Without realising it, by standing so close to the ponies and trying to manage their every step, while worrying about them 'getting away', they're inadvertently unnerving the ponies.

'It's OK, they'll catch up,' I say. 'Let's keep walking.'

While continuing to walk along can generate more anxiety in new pony walkers with the increasing distance, the ponies themselves become more relaxed as the 'pressure' reduces. Ponies can, of course, pick up very well on what people are feeling. Having someone at your elbow saying, 'Come on, come on, no don't stop, come on,' – at each step can be perplexing for them. Their usual response is to stop and look quizzical, as if to say, 'What's wrong? Is there something to worry about?' Or otherwise, they do what we often do when someone nags us: shut out that noise, making them less responsive.

The liberty walks offer an opportunity for the ponies to take responsibility for themselves, express themselves and enjoy being somewhere different. It's all about building mutual trust, respect and understanding – and learning about 'horse time' as distinct from 'human time'.

People who come out with us more than once are generally more relaxed on the second walk, and they're rewarded with more responsive, relaxed ponies.

Top left: Millie and Monsieur Chapeau at Horner Water.

Top right: Nadine and Gunde from Germany enjoy a liberty walk with Monsieur Chapeau.

Centre, left to right: Monty exploring the terrain;

Millie with Monsieur Chapeau and Monty;

June with Pumpkin and Monsieur Chapeau;

Millie bonding with the ponies at liberty.

Far left: 'Uncle' Harry with June.

Left: Monsieur Chapeau loves exploring the forest.

Monsieur Chapeau and Monty make new friends.

Making the rendevous for the Exmoor National Park Authority Archaeological Walk.

It's also interesting to see initially rather apprehensive ponies who can be sharp and reactive at the beginning of a walk, significantly mellowing and chilling towards the end as they get the idea – and realise how enjoyable it is. Both ponies and people can learn and develop through these walks – within this unique horse/human herd situation. Unsurprisingly, the ability to happily communicate and come along on a liberty walk translates very well when the ponies are ridden and we've moved to routinely using comfortable bitless bridles like the Australian Light Rider and Transcend.

Re-discovering Pack Horse Trails of Exmoor

In August, we took part in an Archaeological Pack Horse Walk with Exmoor Ponies, as part of the MEPBG's Heritage Exmoor Pony Festival. Led by Exmoor National Park Authority's Rob Wilson-North, the plan was to follow the ancient pack horse trails that cross Exmoor in the Ley Hill (Horner Gate) area. Starting from Crawter Hill, south of Porlock, we'd explore an abandoned medieval village and its fields, open moorland and meander through the upper parts of Horner Wood. Monsieur Chapeau and Monty were nominated for the job.

The two ponies were groomed, loaded in the trailer and ready to go when a cacophony of the 4x4's alarms went off and all efforts to silence them were rebuffed, sending our nerves jangling and having goodness knows what effect on the previously calm ponies. Eventually, Nick managed to stop

Above left: Both ponies comfortable and relaxed with their new 'herd' for the day.

Above right: Enjoying the spectacular views across Exmoor towards the Quantock Hills at Horner Gate.

the noise but then the vehicle itself refused to start. Time was running tight to make the rendezvous for the walk. Having been advertised as 'accompanied by Exmoor ponies', the ponies simply had to get there. With that special efficiency that farmers have, Nick swapped vehicles and we were soon on our way and fortunately arrived just as the walkers were gathering. Monsieur Chapeau and Monty stepped calmly out from the trailer as if butter wouldn't melt, to receive much fuss and attention.

Both ponies behaved impeccably on the walk and were good with the people, some of whom had little or no experience of horses. Their presence seemed to dissolve any awkwardness between the walkers and soon everyone was happily chatting with each other with a positive buzz. As we paused at each point of interest and to admire the spectacular Exmoor views, Monsieur Chapeau and Monty quickly worked out that these were ideal opportunities to graze. Meandering at a pace to suit the slowest walkers, the ponies were behaving much as they would out on the moor, migrating from location to location, grazing as they went along. The actual pack horse trails were deeply entrenched, having been formed by many hooves and feet over the years and, chatting with Rob, we thought how good it would be if we could re-discover more of the original trails and get Exmoor ponies walking them again. At the end of the walk, the happy smiling faces and enthusiastic appreciation for Monsieur Chapeau and Monty showed this was a great way of connecting people with Exmoor and the ponies.

What struck me about the day was how well the Exmoor ponies had dealt with the experience. Not so much as 'obedient ponies on leads' but as interested, sentient creatures, who were comfortable with a group of strangers. Monty and Monsieur Chapeau had calmly accepted their new 'herd' for the day and happily walked in a place they'd never been before, with people milling all around them. The walkers had responded accordingly and I wondered if we'd all benefited from being part of Monsieur Chapeau and Monty's herd for a time.

Monty enjoying attention at the end of the walk.

Chapter Seven
Bear's Family Herd

The stallion as a family man – and summer events

In mid August, we were blessed with the arrival of Bear and Maisie's beautiful colt foal, who we named Kilimanjaro. As always with Maisie's foals, he appeared effortlessly in those secretive early hours and surprised me when I went to see the ponies first thing in the morning. Now very experienced at watching the arrival of his foals, Bear stood proudly nearby, careful not to approach until Maisie allowed him to greet the foal when she felt it was appropriate. This time around, she was far more relaxed about the introductions and they were soon all together as a cohesive little herd.

Summer pony events bring visitors to the farm
During August, we held some Wild Pony Whispering workshops and, a few days after Kilimanjaro was born, we had an open afternoon for our Exmoor Pony Project and the moorland breeders group. With various demo/viewing areas and displays, along with refreshments in our threshing barn, there was

Top: Bear, Maisie and Kilimanjaro.

Above: Tender moments with his son.

Left: Kilimanjaro loves to shadow his father as much as possible.

Opposite: Bear with Maisie and Kilimanjaro after giving his liberty demo.

67

Maisie and Kilimanjaro at our Open Afternoon

From top: Bear and Heather Williams (Mum);

Tom Faggus with Caitlin Gubb-Fradgley;

Monty and Topaz at the Open Afternoon with June;

Dawn and Bear demonstrating at a Wild Pony Whispering workshop.

plenty to see. The event was supported by local photographers and artists (Jamie and Lisa Waters, Maureen Harvey, Helen South and Helen Disberry), moorland farmers and pony enthusiasts. An array of cakes and refreshments were coordinated by my mother Heather Williams and Sue Downes and there was welcome help from June Eckhart, Alyson Govier, Gareth Latham, Peter Hotchkiss, Millie Ker, Sue Byrne, Maria Floyd, Matthew Coldicutt, Kate South, James Bryant, Kate Hele and Oliver Lock and others.

The ponies were curious and engaging with visitors, including three year old Tom Faggus, who was spotted carefully sniffing noses with young Caitlin Gubb-Fradgley. His willing, trusting connection was lovely to see in a pony who has struggled to trust people. Children have a wonderful ability to connect with authentic good intention and Tom clearly liked that a lot. He also proved keen to interact with people at our pony workshops. If he liked the look of someone, he'd wander up and carefully stand next to them, waiting for some attention. This year, he has flourished within the herd, at first hiding behind the other ponies, and then emerging to progress when he feels comfortable to do so. Certainly for him, the value of learning within a settled herd has been an enormous help.

Bear, Maisie and Kilimanjaro

As Bear's son Kilimanjaro had arrived only a few days before our open afternoon, I was wondering how Maisie and the foal would cope with visitors keen to see stallion Bear – and inevitably, the new foal. We gave them a large part of the barn to meander around, with a private area if Maisie felt she needed to remove the foal from view. There we could monitor their responses and turn them back out into the field if necessary. Our visitors were all thankfully very careful and quiet when they entered the barn. Bear stood proudly and Kilimanjaro showed a cautious interest in the new people, while Maisie

Kilimanjaro likes to watch and mirror everything his father does.

watched the proceedings closely, ensuring that her foal remained just out of touching distance. The three of them did a wonderful PR job for Exmoor ponies that afternoon.

An immense bond between father and son

Kilimanjaro developed an immediate and adoring relationship with his father. Bear soon had a little shadow who followed him around, watching everything he did and trying to copy his every move. Not long after the open day, I moved the three of them into a field where they'd also have access to the barn and agility obstacles, giving Bear the opportunity to patrol interesting new boundaries and get some good exercise. Participants in my pony workshops were able to observe the nurturing, interactive relationships within this small family herd that included a stallion. This is not something seen too often with our modern horse management systems, where it is still commonplace to keep stallions isolated. On one afternoon workshop, Bear gave a demonstration of his agility skills in the barn, with Maisie and Kilimanjaro looking on. It was fascinating to then see the natural interactions between Bear and Kilimanjaro as the stallion chose to explore some of the obstacles with his son, at liberty.

Bonding with Kilimanjaro.

The little foal has learned to push the giant ball, walk through the drums, walk over tarpaulin and play with the strands of the flapping curtain. Learning to deal with unexpected stimulus, going over, under and through curious objects – without fear – is a fantastic introduction to developing the right attitude and confidence for a future performance pony. While the mother nurtures, feeds and protects her foals, it is often the stallion who teaches them to explore and play – with incredible tenderness and tolerance.

This small family herd offered us some wonderful insights into the role of stallions, and to better understand how the foals running out on the moor in the free-living herds must benefit enormously from the presence of their fathers.

A poignant moment occurred during a workshop when Bear and Maisie started grooming each other, while Kilimanjaro suckled his mother – a sight I'm sure no-one will forget in a hurry and beautifully captured on camera by artist Rebecca de Mendonca.

Kilimanjaro and Maisie greeting workshop visitors.

Chapter Eight

The Untouchable Stallion

His owner's death leaves a magnificent pony in need of help – can the herd provide it?

For the past year, Charlie and Anne Whittle had been looking after and working to secure good futures for a significant number of ponies belonging to a keen Exmoor pony enthusiast, Hilary Williams, who had sadly died the previous summer. All of the ponies had to be found new homes and as various of them were not completely socialised, this was not easy. The ponies were all in good health – Hilary had provided every possible convenience for them, including lovely paddocks, plentiful water troughs, shelter, good boundaries and secure gates. Nick and I and others, assisted where we could and slowly, solutions were found, but there was one pony who presented a particular challenge. He was a beautiful four-year-old stallion who would not accept any handling at all. Extremely wary, he spun away from anyone attempting to approach him, however quietly. A further problem was that he had failed the physical inspection, apparently for a pale foot, so he could not be a pedigree registered Exmoor, take part in breed showing classes, or obtain a stallion licence to breed. This limited his appeal and opportunities. He was stunningly handsome, but he couldn't remain entire. Charlie and Anne, who are long-standing and experienced Exmoor pony breeders and producers, managed to first sedate him through a feed, which allowed the vet near enough to put him under anaesthetic and geld him – and he recovered well from that. The question was – what to do with this wild-natured pony whose resistance to being touched did not diminish after his gelding?

As fortune would have it, the people who bought Hilary's property decided to offer a permanent home to the three remaining ponies – but they too were wary of the gelding. Anne and Charlie were hesitant to put him into a normal stable or livery situation, where it was felt he was likely to have difficulty settling.

We already had a large number of ponies at the farm and our remit so far had been to help foals born on the moor. But I had watched the wild-natured pony with interest and felt that he could respond well to our approach. Hilary had been an enthusiastic supporter of our work and she had also given years of help to moorland breeders. I knew that Hilary's pony must come to us. It was the very least we could do for her.

Top: The gelding ready to load.

Above: Arriving at his new home.

Opposite: Handsome, proud ... and untouchable.

71

He had never travelled anywhere before, so some thought had to go into loading this untouchable pony. Nick positioned the trailer and ramp to create a short 'corridor' from the corral – offering him a natural direction to go up inside. Anne gently herded him from the field into the corral and we stood quietly as he trotted around, snorting and posturing – and staring wildly about. It was imperative that we remained calm and unconcerned, with low energy. Soon, he paused and looked at me. The anxious but contemplative expression in his eyes told me he was assessing the situation. It was natural that his adrenaline was up, contained here in the corral with people he didn't know well. But he was thinking and processing instead of panicking and I knew that I would be able to successfully work with this pony.

Soon, he walked up the ramp and into the trailer where he stood quietly, rather than banging and crashing around. We set off on the short journey across the vale and on the way up to the farm, paused for a few minutes to see the big herd. The gelding gave a call from the trailer and received a number of calls and whickers back from the herd. He was then quiet. Something had passed between him and the other ponies which we could tangibly sense. Back at the farm, we reversed the trailer into the corral and let down the ramp. The wild-natured Exmoor was alone and in a different environment for the first time in his life. He leapt down the ramp and trotted around the corral and was soon tucking into a bowl of feed.

'He's alright. He's going to settle down here,' said Charlie.

The gelding had a curious name on his passport that didn't lend itself to daily use, and we had no idea if he had a nickname. What to call him? With his dashing good looks, dramatic nature and slightly wild and reckless approach to life, a name sprang to mind which resonated with everyone. So D'Artagnan it was.

Taking in his new surroundings.

The taming of D'Artagnan

After giving D'Artagnan time to take stock of his new environment, I felt that it was important to establish a connection with him on this first day. He had shown me that what he feared most was the idea of a human within his zone of pressure (the area immediately surrounding him). This had been exacerbated during the year when the ponies had been without their owner Hilary, and he seemed to be the most affected of all the ponies by her loss. For this reason, I did not want to keep him contained in a stable and on his own because I felt it would increase his anxiety. Yet if I turned him out with other ponies right away – without achieving some kind of an understanding – he would simply 'hide' behind the others and evade me.

So how to approach this? As various people had already tried to patiently get near him, without success, I felt inclined to try something completely different and introduce him to the idea of protected contact (for him), to help dissolve his phobia of being touched.

How protected contact can help with confidence issues

Nick and I let D'Artagnan into the big barn, so he could get used to being with us in a contained but large space – and let him settle. He explored the barn and maintained exactly the same distance from us as outside. After a while I opened the door of the pen area, which is the size of a generous stable, and gently encouraged him in with a handful of feed in a bowl. Here, contained in a smaller space, he was initially more agitated. I left the pen and he calmed again. However, when I quietly re-entered the pen, D'Artagnan made it immediately clear that being in this closer proximity with me was completely unacceptable for him and I had to make a rapid exit, for my own safety. Maintaining this agitated state when anyone got anywhere near him was no good for either him or us. It was dangerous. When I left the pen, he immediately calmed down. We had to try and establish a calmer and more confident way of doing things.

Despite his rather erratic behaviour, I felt that underneath the frenetic surface was a very intelligent chap who had just lost his confidence in people after the loss of his owner.

'He calms so quickly,' I said to Nick. 'This pony is ready for me to show him that he has nothing to fear from being touched. But that first touch is not going to come in an open space. He needs protected contact – from me.'

It's a strange concept to accept that an animal we want to help can feel that they need protecting from us, when we mean them absolutely no harm. We sometimes have to subdue our own egos to understand it from their point of view. The very worst thing to do to a pony like D'Artagnan is to 'rope' them. Throwing a rope over a pony like this and 'establishing an understanding' is force and coercion. It may eventually subdue him, but it is in the manner of someone rushing across the room and grabbing you – rather than politely introducing themselves. What I needed to do was get close to D'Artagnan without hands on physical restraint of any kind. That first touch needed to be light – and it must not exacerbate his fear.

I quietly re-entered his pen and made my way around to open the door into the handling shute that is set up at one side of it. D'Artagnan stood at the other side of the pen, staring intently at me. As I moved away from the shute, he moved closer towards it, maintaining the maximum distance possible from me. He looked into it and decided he'd rather be in there than in the pen with me. Realising he couldn't go through, he looked alert, but he didn't back out. I gently closed the door so

D'Artagnan willingly enters, maintaining a 'safe' distance from us all the time – Nick shows passive body language.

The 'untouchable' D'Artagnan finds the confidence to be touched through gentle interactions and 'protected contact' (for him).

D'Artagnan meeting Monsieur Chapeau and his new herd.

he was inside the shute and let him process this. He didn't panic. In fact, he was already calmer than when he and I had been standing inside the pen together. I took my trusty feather duster and standing outside the shute, gently stroked him with it and he accepted it. He was already an amazingly different pony from the one a few minutes before. I replaced the feather duster with my hand and gently stroked him from the rump over his back, over his wither and then up his neck. He turned his head slowly towards me and sniffed my hand. Then we sniffed noses.

Nick was surprised when I picked up a head collar.

'It feels right,' I said.

D'Artagnan let me drape the head collar over his wither, do up the neck strap, then move it up his neck and fasten the strap over his nose. Again, he turned his head to me rather than away and there was no tension or starting. There he was, standing quietly in the shute, allowing me to stroke him and wearing a head collar, calm and accepting. I quietly slipped it off again and let him out. He walked away across the barn, still wanting to maintain that distance in the open area, but in a more relaxed way. D'Artagnan had done so well and it was important that he was rewarded. Keeping him on his own in this strange new environment was not a reward. He needed turnout in the pasture, and some new friends. Monsieur Chapeau would of course be essential to his new group. I also wanted to include Prince Kailash, Tom Faggus and Baluran, who all needed some one to one handling. Leaving D'Artagnan with some haylage to munch, we set off to bring the big herd back from their summer grazing fields.

Introducing D'Artagnan to his new companions

The big herd was about as far away as they could be, up on their favourite humpy area – literally dots in the distance. I called across to them from the gate and they came cantering back up to the farm.

Walking among the herd, I quietly picked up a connection with the ponies who I wanted to follow me to the paddock that adjoined the corral where D'Artagnan was waiting. Monsieur Chapeau came first, followed by Tom Faggus. Imperial Topaz realised something was going on and presented himself with enthusiasm, 'Me too!' he seemed to be saying. A little careful herding soon had the elusive Prince Kailash and his older brother Baluran in the paddock and to my delight, veteran babysitter Uncle Otis decided this was a situation that should also involve him. I had my team.

It didn't take long before the geldings migrated across the paddock and discovered the new pony in the adjacent corral. Monsieur Chapeau was the first to approach and drew himself up to his full height with a display of impressive airs. One by one, the others came over. D'Artagnan remained at the gate – careful and wary. After each of the geldings had greeted him and some had gone off to graze, I decided to let D'Artagnan out with them.

Otis, the eldest at twelve years, voiced the most objection to the newcomer and the younger ponies stood back while D'Artagnan and Otis 'conversed'. Although there was much posturing and backing into each other, they did not want to actually hurt each other – this was all about establishing their positions in the group. Each gelding took it in turns to push D'Artagnan out and away from the

Squaring up with Otis and working his way into the gelding herd.

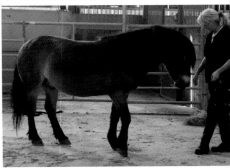

group. But each time he returned into the middle of them and started grazing, clearly saying, 'I'm in this herd, get used to it.' Rather like Penelope had done when she and Pierre Parfait had joined the main herd. His persistence paid off, because the geldings were soon all grazing together.

It was the best possible outcome for D'Artagnan on his first day with us. He had new companions to think about, rather than being all alone in a strange place. I knew we'd build a much better bond with this highly sensitive pony by allowing him his liberty and not shutting him in a stable. Understanding how to compassionately use 'protected contact' – and avoiding actual hands on physical restraint – had enabled me to offer him far more liberty on his first day with us, than would likely have been extended to him with a more 'conventional' approach to handling.

Not long afterwards, D'Artagnan started tentatively allowing me to stroke and groom him and put on his head collar out in the open barn area. His temperament remains 'dramatic' and he can spin and veer away at the slightest movement, so I have to ensure I approach him softly and gently. He watches my every move with intensity – yet radiating from him is the desire to connect, with the wariness of a wild deer! He is also like this with the other ponies – and they notice it. His nervy reactiveness can annoy them and he often gets a nip or lunge from one of the others, particularly the more dominant mares. His tense behaviour disturbs the herd's equilibrium, because calmness means safety in a herd, and raised adrenaline means danger. By over-reacting and remaining in a state of nervous tension, D'Artagnan causes the herd to remain alert – for no good reason – and they don't like it. The other ponies are going to help enormously with D'Artagnan's development. He is still only four years old and has a great deal to learn. Fortunately for him, he is now amongst a herd of willing teachers who can help him find his confidence again.

D'Artagnan accepting a head collar in the barn and exploring agility objects with his herd.

Tom Faggus also preferred protected contact initially.

The Feet of Tom Faggus

At three years old, Tom Faggus has now been off the moor for two years. Yet he had retained a self-protective wariness that reminds me never to take the Exmoor's cooperation and compliance for granted. He has taught me infinite patience and it was Tom who showed me that he preferred 'protected contact' in the shute to overcome his fear of being touched. However, the very first pony to introduce us to the original idea of 'protected contact' was Penelope Pitstop, who as a wild-born newly-weaned foal some years ago, was adept at spinning around and delivering lightning kicks when I stood in a stable with her. As you can imagine, I wasn't too fond of this. We scratched our heads for a while, not wanting to 'grab' or restrain Penelope, but needing to progress her handling. She appeared to have a clear 'no-go' zone around her which she wasn't willing to negotiate. So Nick created a gate that swung back into the corner of the stable, which we padded with horse rugs. We then gently guided Penelope to walk into the corner of the stable where we could slowly bring the gate around and reduce the space, until she was happy to stand quietly behind it, with me the other side. With that 'protected contact' and without being 'grabbed' it took only a very short period of stroking her before she allowed me to put on her head collar. Penelope has never been hard to 'catch' since and she does not kick out any more. Her 'phobia' of anyone coming near to her was dissolved by standing quietly behind the padded gate – and she suffered no stress. Since then we have been fortunate enough to have a proper 'shute'.

This method only applies to some ponies. Most ponies will gradually allow you into their personal space through carefully building trust at liberty, in a larger open area. However, when ponies choose to be defensive, this can be dangerous – as D'Artagnan had demonstrated – and 'protected contact' can be the vital link in trauma-free socialisation.

During the past two years, Tom Faggus had favoured two distinct responses – he would either lunge or he would slowly turn his back end to you and make his intention very clear. Neither of these behaviours was safe or acceptable, so I had taught him to stand in the shute to have his feed, which he accepted happily. Then I stroked him briefly with the feather duster and let him out. These short sessions continued for a while and Tom began to enjoy grooming and then accepting a head collar. When I appeared, he'd walk out from the herd and ask to go in the pen and walk into the shute for his 'session'. All of this then transferred to Tom accepting handling outside the pen and he found the confidence to no longer offer the aggressive behaviours. I truly believe that if this pony's fear had been met with forceful, coercive training – ie, roping, grabbing, hitting, shouting at, etc, – then it would have had disastrous consequences. By ignoring the bad behaviour and looking for a way of progressing communications with Tom, we'd managed to bypass his defensive responses – and enjoyed a wonderful breakthrough.

No foot, on inspection

Although Tom Faggus's parents had already been identified through DNA testing, he hadn't yet had his breed society physical inspection, because he still had to let me pick up his feet. We were not prepared for Tom to be physically restrained to have his feet forced up to look underneath them. Not only would it be very dangerous to attempt this with a strapping three-year-old Exmoor, but also because we believe this can trigger unnecessary behavioural issues – particularly with Tom! Fortunately, Tom had worn his feet very well naturally, but at three years old, he also needed to accept a rasp now and again. Because he could be defensive, any co-operation had to be won by building trust, not by demanding compliance. If he didn't like something, Tom still gave some very clear signs that he was thinking about defending himself. The way forwards was to work with him in a way where he learned not to resort to showing that kind of behaviour when feeling uncertain. So I had taken things slowly with him. The reward was steady, increasing improvement and the gradual emergence of a more confident and affectionate Tom Faggus.

He was now used to accepting a head collar and grooming and I could progress to stroking down his legs, lightly touching his feet and then requesting him to briefly lift each one. At first, he produced a robust stamp but over time, this became a reluctant lift without quite so much attitude – and eventually, a brief hold. Tom Faggus had at last allowed me to willingly pick up all his feet. Sometimes a pony appears in your life to remind you that you can be better, more patient and that you're still not seeing enough 'detail' in your horse communications. Tom Faggus is a Professor in this subject!

The gradual emergence of a more confident and affectionate Tom Faggus.

Chapter Nine

An Unwelcome Night-Time Adventure

One dark night we woke to something that put the big herd to the ultimate test

One dark night in September, we had gone to bed when I was woken by a loud noise – there is no mistaking the roar of a mature stallion. The dogs had been barking sporadically, but farm dogs often do that at night as they respond to foxes, stags, other dogs in the vale and myriad wild creatures. There were two more roars in quick succession and both Nick and I leapt out of bed. Something was up.

As we opened the back door to the yard, we were met with little Lady Martha staring in at us. Behind her were various other ponies and blinking into the blackness beyond, I could just make out more moving shadows. There were a lot of ponies milling around and this was not good, because the herd should have been safely enclosed in their group of fields, well away from the farm. Their arrival in the yard meant they had all been out on the lanes in the dead of night.

'Oh my God, they're out,' I stated the obvious. The most pressing issue to deal with was Bear. Fairly agitated by the arrival of all these ponies, he was talking to a number of them over the gate. A five bar gate is no barrier for an Exmoor stallion motivated to get out so we quickly persuaded him, Maisie and their foal Kilimanjaro to go into the barn where they were safely contained while we worked out what had happened – and what to do about it.

The black, cloudy night meant it was impossible to clearly see how many ponies were here and who was still missing. Monsieur Chapeau, D'Artagnan and the group of geldings were taking great interest in the proceedings from their own paddock and I was thankful that they at least weren't amongst the escapees. Forcing myself to stay calm, I greeted the ponies nearest to me and asked them to draw to me and follow me. They did. Calling softly to the others, I started to lead them across the yard, past the farm machinery and to a corral and field that weren't being used. I had no head collars, ropes or feed. This was an emergency and now, the strength of my connection with the herd would be put fully to the test. The various shadows started to drift towards me and I could feel their apprehension. It was essential that I presented myself as the safest place to be, adrenaline low and offering them a strong and pure energy connection to follow me – right now. Their night vision is way better than ours, so while I was struggling to see them, they would find it much easier to see me. Walking confidently to the corral, I had some ponies right with me and others I could hear making

Opposite: The big herd faced a challenge no horse owner wants to experience.

their way behind us. Opening the gate I walked in and encouraged them to follow. They did – every single one of the ponies who had come up to the farm followed me in. But a significant number were still missing. Including the foal Pierre Parfait and his mother Penelope Pitstop, and our three Arabian horses.

At this point, we had no idea where or how they'd got out. We drove down the lane to their fields and the top gates nearest the farm were firmly shut. As were the gates further down. They must have got out through a lower gate in one of the farthest fields. Driving past the cottages and onward, we finally discovered the problem. An open swinging gate onto the lane. But this rarely used gate was extremely stiff to open and its structure meant there was no way the ponies could push it open from inside the field. There was no footpath through this field and it was the middle of the night. We realised that someone had deliberately – and maliciously – opened the gate. I felt sickened that anyone would let horses and ponies out onto the roads where they and others could come to harm.

Nick dropped me off a little further down the lane, where there was open access onto a number of arable fields. If the herd had been driven down there, it was likely they'd have cantered into these fields, rather than continue down the narrow lane towards the main road – herd animals will usually look for open rather than contained spaces when taking flight. He then drove back up to do a sweep of the fields and see if any ponies were left inside.

Left alone, I called out into the darkness and listened. But there was silence. Not a hint of movement or response on this dark, still night. I could see droppings on the road so knew that a large number of ponies, and possibly our horses, had passed this way.

Nick returned with the welcome news that Penelope Pitstop and Pierre Parfait had remained in the field, as had Anstey Princess and her yearling daughter Black Bess. Such wise mares to understand that leaving the fields at night was too dangerous and they had overcome their herd instincts to protect their young. With them safely shut in the field, we followed the trail of droppings down the lane.

'In all my years here, I've never known stock to reach the main road,' Nick reassured me. 'There are too many alternative places for them to go.'

The droppings stopped well before we reached the main road and indicated that at some point, the ponies had turned around and gone back up the hill. After continuing on and checking the roads for a distance in each direction, we were satisfied that none of them had come this way. Heading back up to the farm, we stopped periodically to listen and call out. But only an eerie silence greeted us.

'Let's see if anyone else has arrived back in the yard,' said Nick.

Throughout all of this, he had remained completely calm, as seasoned stock farmers do. It had a positive effect on my own demeanour. There was no-one to greet us on this first visit back, so we headed out again, around the lanes. Thankfully, all around us on the estate are open areas, so the horses and ponies had myriad places to explore and graze. With the thick cloud obscuring the moon, it was very difficult for us to see into any of the fields. There were also areas leading into the

Recovering the herd.

moorland, where they could get off the lanes, at least until they met a deer gate or fencing. We kept searching and returning to the farm. At this time of night, the lanes were also thankfully, completely devoid of traffic.

'They'll return soon,' said Nick, with more confidence than I felt, but I knew he was right.

Sure enough, not long afterwards, the dogs started barking and we found the remainder of the herd walking up the drive – including the Arabian horses. Again, I asked them to draw to me and follow me to safety. Thankfully, they did and were clearly very glad to be home. At first light, we brought the two mares and youngsters up to the farm and soon the whole herd was together again.

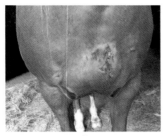

Matara is injured.

Matara is injured

Checking everyone over for possible injury, there was some superficial lameness – likely to be caused by pounding the lanes – the odd knock, and a few cuts and scrapes. But it was Matara the Arabian mare who bore the brunt of the injuries and who through that, offered clues about what had happened. I was horrified to see that she was not only lame but had a massive haematoma on her chest. In the middle of it was a deepish cut that looked like something had entered the flesh at an angle. Chilled, I realised that if it had hit her 'head on', it could have been far more serious. That didn't bear thinking about. Puzzled as to what had caused her injury, I remembered the field gate that we had found swinging out into the lane. The open gate partially blocked the route up the lane towards the farm, and it was clear from the droppings that at least some of the herd had initially travelled down the hill towards the main road – at some speed. But the trail of droppings had abruptly stopped, indicating that they had turned to come back up. It's likely that the adrenaline-levels within this group, containing three highly-sensitive Arabians, had caused them to canter, or at least trot briskly back up the lane and with a group of them trying to get past the swinging gate, perhaps Matara had run into it, causing the sticking out bolt to pierce her chest at an angle. The sheer force of hitting the gate could well have resulted in the haematoma. If this had been the case, it would likely have given her – and the others – a terrible fright and sent them into flight, which could explain why they'd run off somewhere, returning later than the other ponies.

Matara looked very sorry for herself and I had no hesitation in calling the vet, who provided antibiotics and anti-inflammatory treatment to encourage the haematoma to drain. Infection was a risk so she had to remain closely monitored for the next week or so. Another of our Arabian horses, Padric, had a nasty cut to his leg. So I separated the horses off from the rest of the herd. The incident was, of course, reported to the police.

Once satisfied that everyone else was OK, we let the ponies back down into their summer grazing and Nick bought a number of chains and padlocks. It is now a sad fact that locked gates are a requirement. It had been a nasty experience. However, there is some good to be found in everything and we had learned something valuable from the ordeal. The herd, when let out and frightened, had wanted to come home. They wanted to seek us out, led by little Lady Martha – and when they found us, they wanted to connect and let me lead them to safety. I was so proud of them all.

Top: Sadly locked gates became a necessity.

Above: The Arabians, Matara, Padric and Casper, were later able to return to the big herd.

Chapter Ten
Pack Pony Protest Walk

Exmoors and Dartmoors take a stand against pony meat for the dinner table

In early autumn, Monsieur Chapeau and Monty had another interesting walk to take part in. We were to join Sam Goodwin and his Dartmoor Pack Ponies as they travelled from Dartmoor to Exmoor and back again, protesting about using semi-feral pony meat for the dinner table. Currently, in the UK, horses and ponies are not classed as 'agricultural animals' for the food chain. They enjoy a different status to animals farmed for their meat, such as cattle (beef), sheep (lamb), pigs (pork) and chickens (poultry), etc. If equines enter the food chain as 'Animals We Eat', then this special status will be lost – forever – and many feel it could have severe negative implications for overall equine welfare in this country. While the arguments for conservation pony meat schemes as a way of managing numbers have some practical merit, the implications for the status and welfare of those pony breeds, and equines generally, present too many dangers and ethical issues to warrant going down this road – in my opinion. It's fair to say that civilisation has been built on the back of the horse, along with many other magnificent animals, like oxen. The difference is that many of those other animals are now widely perceived as 'food' and horses and ponies are not. I feel they deserve more than ending up on our modern dinner tables. I'd already appeared on a BBC Inside Out programme, putting the opposing view to farming ponies for this purpose and Nick and I decided to support Sam's walk by joining a section of it with some Exmoor ponies – along with Exmoor Pony Project supporters June Eckhart, Alyson Govier, Millie Ker and Peter Rae.

Sam and his three Dartmoor pack ponies were trekking through the days and camping out in the

Monsieur Chapeau and June cross the River Barle – but it's deeper than expected.

Dartmoors and Exmoors meet at Horsen Farm.

Opposite: Sam Goodwin and his Dartmoor pack ponies navigate Horsen Ford.

Monsieur Chapeau watches us cross the river.

Monty thankfully remembers how to be ridden.

open countryside each night. The ponies carried everything needed in their packs and it was going to test their stamina to make this long journey. Various supporters joined Sam for different legs of the walk and we planned to meet him at Horsen Farm on Exmoor and walk along the Barle River Valley into Simonsbath. Monsieur Chapeau and Monty would not be wearing packs and as it turned out, that proved to be very useful.

Crossing a swollen River Barle

The previous night, Sam had endured a heavy rain storm camping out on Molland Moor, which would try the toughest souls, and we were relieved that the weather had lightened to blustery showers as we arrived at Horsen Farm. The Dartmoors and Exmoors were introduced and everyone seemed quietly accepting of this newly formed 'herd'. We set off and discovered that the rain had swelled the River Barle, which was running at quite a depth over Horsen Ford. Still safe to cross, it was nevertheless well over the tops of long boots, as June discovered when she and Monsieur Chapeau walked across. Brave June didn't flinch as her boots disappeared under water in the middle of the crossing – but it caused me to pause. We had not long started out and there were at least a couple of hours of moorland walking before we reached our destination. Dry feet were to be valued and I was also wearing my Dubarry's – many will understand this dilemma.

Monty had only been ridden very lightly. The time resource required by our moorland foal project meant that the wonderful, meandering trail rides of previous years had unfortunately been few and far between for me, while my time was spent taming, training and looking after the increased number of ponies. I looked at Monty.

'Monty, the river is deep and I really don't want to get my feet wet. Do you remember how to be a ridden pony?' Monty's steadfast gaze told me he probably did. I assessed the situation. Here we were, with Monty in a basic bitless bridle (not unlike a head collar) and lead rope, with no saddle, facing a rather swollen river crossing. How much did I want dry socks? A lot.

I stroked Monty across his back and down over the rump and gently leaned over him. I jumped up and down a bit beside him and he stood there, looking back at me as if to say, 'You people are weird but it's OK.' Then I looped the lead rope around his neck to make some makeshift reins and quietly slipped onto his back, letting him process what I was doing, before I slipped off again. He didn't seem to mind at all. All seemed good.

I unfortunately didn't have a riding hat and I would always advocate wearing one, of course. However, if something untoward happened today, I would be landing in the water rather than on a hard surface – and there were also no stirrups to catch my feet in. I sat on Monty bareback once again.

'OK Monty, let's go across and see Monsieur Chapeau.' At the water's edge, I let him peer into its depths, have a splash about a bit and get used to it all. Then he carefully picked his way through the large stones and waded across and up the other side – past Monsieur Chapeau, who was watching in fascination. Monty was very pleased with himself and my socks were dry, unlike poor June.

Later on during the walk, we had to squeeze along a narrow, slippery stone ledge, where the edge

Making our way towards Cow Castle, along the Barle.

dropped straight into a deep part of the river. Sam couldn't risk taking the Dartmoors along it with their wide packs, but unencumbered Monty and Monsieur Chapeau could navigate it with ease. Instead, Sam and his three ponies waded across the river and through a meadow the other side, before crossing back to meet us. Watching him changing his soaking socks and sorting out his ponies caused me to ponder how gruelling the historic pack pony trekking must have been, tackling tough terrain day after day, in all weathers, heavily laden with vital supplies. For us, joining in just for this stunning section of the walk and our Exmoors free of packs – it was all about fun.

Spirits were high as we approached Simonsbath where we were met with coffee and bagels from more supporters, including Sue Howes and Karen Costelloe. Monsieur Chapeau and Monty did a wonderful PR job for Exmoors as they met and greeted everyone. Sam and his lovely Dartmoor ponies continued on their walk and we loaded up to come home with a strengthened resolve to do more pack pony walks on Exmoor.

Above: Sam re-crossing the river.
Below, left to right:
Approaching Simonsbath;
Monty shows Sam the way;
the ponies and walkers.

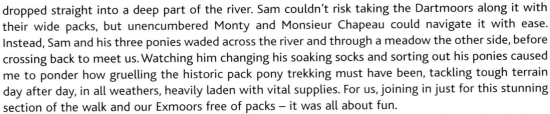

Chapter Eleven

The Exmoor Pony Autumn Gatherings

Excitement, confusion, dismay and joy – the autumn gatherings provide an emotional roller-coaster

In October, we took part in the gathering of the Milton family's historic Herd 23 ponies – the oldest family-owned herd of Exmoor ponies in the world. The herd is split between two locations, with one group of mares running with stallion The Aristocrat (along with young stallion, Coombe Royal, who is learning the ropes) on Withypool Common, and the other group running with stallion Knightoncombe Royal on Anstey Common in Exmoor National Park.

The Withypool Gathering
The team start gathering the Withypool Common ponies from the Westwater side, bringing them across the Sandyway Road and past the farms of Knighton and Brightworthy. The ponies cross the River Barle at Sherdon Hutch, then run up onto Bradymoor, crossing the Landacre Bridge road and then down to the handling pens at the top end of Kitteridge Lane. We'd brought the quad bike and Nick dropped me at Sherdon Hutch crossing where I found a good spot nestled into the bank of the Barle, armed with camera and flask to wait for the ponies to cross. While I was there some paratroopers had picked this very day to march down over Bradymoor and cross the river as part of an endurance walk – and their various ways of navigating it provided some unexpected entertainment.

Finally, I heard cantering hooves and made ready to photograph the ponies. As they reached the river, the stallion and some of his mares stopped midway across to calmly take a drink and ponder the situation, before continuing to migrate up and over Bradymoor. They gazed at me sitting in the river bank and, for a few moments, I felt a wonderful connection with them – immensely moved by their serenity and majesty. Following behind the ponies on horseback were Rex Milton's wife, Banger, and their daughter Rosie – and then Nick arrived to pick me up and follow on.

At the pony pens, it was wonderful to see this magnificent herd at close quarters, and appreciate their striking bright reddish and golden colouring. Charismatic stallion The Aristocrat made it very clear that he was not impressed to have the younger stallion, Coombe Royal, at such close proximity and before entering the pens, drove off the youngster with some ferocity – reminding everyone present of the wild and independent nature of Exmoor ponies.

Stallion and mares pause for a drink in the Barle.

Opposite: Majestic Herd 23 stallion, The Aristocrat.

Herd 23 mares and foals gathered for weaning.

Top: Banger and Rosie Milton follow the herd on horseback.

Above: Rex and Tim Milton sorting out the ponies.

As the mares and foals were brought through the pen system and weaned, The Aristocrat was let back out. Instead of galloping away, he stayed nearby with some of his mares. They were understandably agitated at being separated from their foals who would now be taken down to the farm to await their inspection and registration as pedigree Exmoor ponies. At one point, young stallion Combe Royal came too near once again, and this time The Aristocrat chased him right away up onto the moor and out of sight. Some minutes later he returned to the pens to wait for the remaining mares. This was a mature stallion who certainly knew the ropes and his status within the herd.

The Herd 23 Exmoor ponies are rare in that they include the dun-coloured, pale-gold and bright red bay shades – some with strikingly blond-tipped manes. Dun-coloured Exmoor ponies, particularly those with a dorsal stripe, are becoming extremely scarce. Brothers Rex and Robin Milton, who inherited the herd from their uncle Fred Milton, are seriously concerned that the paler and redder ponies are being eradicated due to an interpretation of the breed society's 'no white markings' rule to fail foals at inspection for having paler or white sole plates. Foals can fail inspection for even small pale or white patches on the sole of a single foot. The paler and redder-coloured Exmoor ponies can be predisposed to having paler sole plates, or pale patches on sole plates. Loss of pigment can also be caused by the concussion of traversing the uneven and stoney ground – which is not a genetic issue.

The Aristocrat chases off young stallion, Combe Royal.

Some of the moorland farmers feel that forcibly lifting the feet of previously unhandled, feisty wild-born foals to examine their sole plates presents unnecessary health and safety risks to people, as well to the foals themselves. Over the past couple of years, the Moorland Exmoor Pony Breeders Group has asked the Exmoor Pony Society to clarify this rule and request that the feet are no longer picked up during the inspections. However, no decisions had yet been made.

The Anstey Common Gathering

Later in the month, we attended the Anstey Common pony gathering. A team of riders, on horses and bikes, comprising the Milton family and friends, gathered in the spirited Herd 23 ponies. I was once again struck by the bright-reddish colouring amongst the darker ponies – and the quality of the stallion, Knightoncombe Royal. After galloping into the pens with his mares and foals, he stood there radiating presence and quality. The foals were also full of presence, powerfully built and impressively well moving. They really are a beautiful herd of Exmoor ponies.

A strikingly handsome Herd 23 foal.

Traversing Anstey Common during the gathering.

The ponies come off the moor into the pens.

Opposite page, top from left:

Gathering Herd 23 from Anstey Common;

magnificent stallion Knightoncombe Royal coming in with the mares and foals;

a beautiful pale gold/red-coloured Herd 23 foal.

A frustrating failure

When the Herd 23 foals were inspected for their pedigree breed registration, there was much disappointment when a filly foal that Rex Milton considered to be his best bred of the year, failed her inspection for having a pale-coloured sole plate. Under current rules, this meant she could not be registered as a pedigree Exmoor, and would be lost from the breeding gene pool. However, this year Rex Milton decided that he would keep her in the herd and continue to campaign for the rules to be changed.

The Farleywater Gathering – Bear's first wild-born foals come in from the moor

In early October, the South family gathered the Farleywater Herd H67 ponies from Buscombe and we were keen to see the foals sired by Bear. The group of semi-feral mares who had first run with Bear at Farleywater, had then returned to their moorland herd which included stallion Wortleberry. So DNA parentage testing of the foals would be necessary to confirm the sires.

It was a bitterly cold day, reminding us how tough the mares have to be to survive all year round on this beautiful but bleak moorland enclosure. Kate South and her father Ian quietly gathered the herd on their own, with Kate walking behind them to guide the ponies into the pens. It's always impressive to see the connection they have with their ponies – drifting them into a small set of pens from a huge expanse of open moorland. The mares and foals looked in great condition, many with long, flowing manes.

The breed society inspection team arrived, including a vet, to take DNA samples, complete passport silhouettes, microchip and physically inspect the ponies. The foals would now be weaned from their mothers and taken off the moor. It was with a mixture of excitement and sadness that I watched the herd in the pens. This would likely be the last time these colts and fillies saw their mothers.

It is not easy to 'pair up' mares and foals in this kind of medley, as they are apprehensive and restless when freshly gathered in from the moor. Suddenly contained in the pens and surrounded by strangers at close quarters, it is hard for them to settle. It also proved difficult, and in some cases

Bear's first wild-born foals – the Farleywater Herd on Buscombe.

The colt and his mother waiting to be let back out.

Kate South drifts in the Farleywater herd with just fingertip directions.

Opposite, top: Mares and foals entering the pens.

Bottom, left and right:
The mares, newly weaned from their foals, hang around the pens calling to them.

impossible, to read the mares' brands (which are supposed to represent the herd number on the shoulder and an individual pony number on the rump prior to 2012, and a maximum 4-digit ID on the rump since 2012). When older mares are not microchipped and the branded marks can't be read, it can make identifying them very confusing.

Gradually, each foal was separated and inspected, including looking at the underneath of their feet. The vet administered a microchip and a DNA sample was taken.

An impressive-looking colt foal and his mother were run through to a pen where some mares were waiting to be let back out onto the moor. They had both been sprayed with a paint mark number, but it appeared the colt was not going to be inspected?

'Wow! That's a nice colt,' I said.

'He's one of Nigel Floyd's,' I was told. So this mare and foal were thought to be from the Tippbarlake Herd 387, which runs on the adjacent 3000 acres of Brendon Common. Sometimes boundary gates are accidentally left open and can result in ponies migrating onto Buscombe – and vice versa. Managing stock in the wilder areas of Exmoor is not an exact science. The gate to the pen was opened and the mares and the stunning colt foal cantered back out onto the moor.

'Nigel is breeding some lovely foals,' was the general opinion.

As the mares and foals continued to be inspected, a strong-looking and charismatic filly foal came into the pen. She was identified as likely to be a daughter of Bear and named Tanana by Kate South. The Hollick-Blee family, who had come to look at the foals, showed an immediate interest. She passed the inspection and they subsequently collected the filly and took her home a day or two later. I was delighted she was going to such a good home. Kathy Hollick-Blee is accomplished in riding side saddle and show jumping, as well as showing, and she has given impressive side saddle displays on her Exmoor, Mr Mischief. Kathy and Adam also own the mare Farleywater Siren, so Tanana will be in good company.

Kate South and the Farleywater ponies.

Farleywater Sitka and his mother.

A strapping colt foal was identified as a likely Bear foal and named Kenai. He passed inspection and was collected by his new owner, Marion Adams, a few days later. Nick and I were waiting to see the foal of the mare called Foxglove. Kate South and I had watched her with Bear the previous year and commented how good it would be if she produced a colt foal who might show stallion potential. Finally, it was announced that Foxglove and her foal had been identified. We took a look at the colt. He had a strikingly attractive head and Kate named him Farleywater Sitka. I thought the mare looked a little different to how I remembered Foxglove, but as I'd only seen her a few times, at a relative distance, I wasn't exactly sure. Her brand was not readable. We decided to take the colt.

Nick asked Ian South if we could borrow the mare as well for a period. He agreed and the mare and foal were put into a separate pen. There were two reasons for this. Firstly, we wanted to give Sitka a gradual weaning where he could get used to his new life off the moors, with his mother alongside. Secondly, experience has taught us that DNA parentage verification is sometimes not straightforward. Having the mare at our farm in case further DNA sampling was needed was, effectively, belt and braces.

Gentle weaning for a wild-born foal

We returned home for our trailer and when we arrived back at the Buscombe pens, Foxglove and her colt foal were alone in the pens, with various mares hanging around nearby, calling for their foals who had been taken to Farleywater Farm. My heart went out to them. For those mares, that was it – one minute they had their foals and the next minute, they were gone. But it would not be like this for Foxglove. She would be accompanying her foal to our farm, where she could see him settled into his new life off the moor.

What had puzzled me at the inspection was that, Narcissa, a young Farleywater mare who had run with Bear, did not appear to have a foal. When I'd visited Bear and the semi-feral mares in 2015, she had been the one he'd brought all the way up the valley to meet me, and with whom he was clearly besotted. In the hustle and bustle of the pens, and with no apparent foal, Narcissa had been let back out onto the moor in a group of mares. I hadn't even seen her that morning. It remained a mystery for me.

So with three Bear foals physically identified, we now had to wait for the DNA testing to confirm the parentage. The prospects looked good for the Farleywater foals this year, with the 'Bear' foals already sold, and of the others, two going to join another moorland herd, two going to Wales to their new home with John Adams, and some remaining at Farleywater to find homes for. Thoughtful breeding programmes and more proactive promotion of the moorland herds was starting to result in better foal sales which is very encouraging.

Below left: Sitka and his mother wait in the pens for us to return with the trailer.

Below right: Stallion Bear and the young mare, Narcissa, who he brought to see me when I visited him running with the Farleywater mares in 2015.

Main: Sitka and his mother settle into life at Holt Ball.
Inset: The mare shows a willingness to engage and trust Dawn very quickly.

Chapter Twelve
A Meeting of Foals

After leading separate lives so far, the paths of Bear's foals were about to cross

Farleywater Sitka and his mother settled in well at our farm. They quickly understood to come into the barn for some haylage or a feed, so there was no problem in giving them immediate 24/7 turnout. I wanted to avoid containing or over-socialising the semi-feral mare, while at the same time establishing a connection with them, so we could get to know the foal and start to ease his transition to his new life. In the event, the mare was immediately engaging and soon happy enough to come up and offer a muzzle to hand greeting (where you offer your hand, palm down and fingers relaxed and wait for the pony to touch it with their nose). She was remarkably calm and accepting of her new routine.

Soon after they arrived, we decided to bring Penelope Pitstop and her foal Pierre Parfait out of the big herd and introduce Pierre to his first colt foal companion.

While meeting a fellow colt foal was a wonderful opportunity for Pierre Parfait, it meant that he had to be separated from his special friend Lady Martha. She was not very happy about this but she soon became closer to the other yearling and two-year-old fillies. I felt sorry for her, but unfortunately, it is inevitable that fillies have to be separated from the colts, until they are gelded.

Pierre Parfait, on the other hand, was delighted with his new chum, Sitka, and they were soon engaged in robust colt play. Penelope Pitstop was not so impressed, shooing away Sitka and remaining aloof and 'dramatic' with Foxglove. The older mare remained calm and careful – years of living out on the moor in a free-living herd, in a challenging environment, had taught her to save energy rather than engage with this kind of behaviour from a younger mare. She neither rose to it or backed away. Not getting the reaction she demanded, Penelope Pitstop began to calm down too.

Curiously, I found it difficult to call Foxglove 'Foxglove'. Each time I said the name it didn't feel right. A sort of intuitive feeling of uneasiness, which I tried to dismiss.

Holtball Kilimanjaro joins the colt herd
In the meantime, Bear's son – young Kilimanjaro – had become rather boisterous. He was acting like a little mirror of his father, copying Bear's behaviours and gestures and thinking it rather fun to

Penelope and Pierre Parfait meeting the new arrivals.

Holtball Kilimanjaro (above far left) had become a little precocious and benefitted enormously from joining his sibling colts.

Above: Kilimanjaro and Maisie meeting the other mares and foals.

Opposite: Colt play – evolving understanding and awareness through play and play-fighting.

challenge and leap about with anyone who came to see him – including me. What Kilimanjaro needed was the help and guidance of some 'aunts' and to meet and socialise with some siblings. Although very cute, he was behaving a little bit like a spoilt child. So while it was sad to separate Kilimanjaro from the father he adored, it would be very good for him to learn to play with other colt foals and hopefully balance his behaviour. As it happened, Kilimanjaro soon found out that he had to think carefully about his interactions with others. Firstly, he discovered that his new aunts were not well disposed to him zooming up and 'bombing' them. Their responses were forthright, sending Kilimanjaro reeling away in shock. He also discovered that his fellow colt foals were all bigger and older than him and he had to think about the way he approached and interacted with them too. He began to appreciate and value his mother immensely. Maisie is a wonderful matriarch and navigates a pasture of mares and foals like a ship in full sail. Kilimanjaro began to make friends with the other colts and they were soon all playing together. Almost overnight, he became a far nicer-mannered colt foal – and once again, the herd had shown me the way.

There is quite a shock
After some weeks, the breed society informed us that DNA testing had concluded that Sitka was not sired by Bear but by the stallion Wortleberry - and that his mother was not Foxglove. The mare was actually Lark, who was a matriarch herself at the grand age of 19. This explained a lot. While I was disappointed that we did not have the Bear son we had wanted, it explained my nagging intuitive feeling that the mare was not Foxglove. In my mind's eye, she was not the shape of the Foxglove I had seen the previous year and she hadn't 'felt' like Foxglove. I had even more respect for Lark now, that she had accepted her new routine with us so gracefully, having lived wild and free for 19 years. She is also the mother of three-year-old Farleywater Dazzler, who runs with our big herd. This news also explained why Sitka was taller and rangier than a typical Bear foal, so we were not entirely surprised. However, the mystery remained as to the whereabouts of Foxglove and her foal. Where were they? No one knew.

Sitka is not sired by Bear.

Members of the big herd convey their feelings to D'Artagnan (who is squaring up on the right here).

Chapter Thirteen

The Big Herd Comes Home

With winter approaching, it's time for a return to the farm and merging of herds

D'Artagnan and his group of ponies were progressing well up at the farm. However, the nights were now closing in, it was getting colder and wetter and it was time to bring the big herd up from the summer pasture and introduce D'Artagnan to a lot more new friends. Calling them home, the horses and ponies were connected, responsive, willing – and joyful. A gregarious, positive energy radiated from them. They looked the picture of health and fitness – their freer and more spacious summer and autumn routine had suited them well – from youngsters to veterans.

D'Artagnan and his companions were grazing in the home paddock. Here, everyone could greet each other and there was plenty of room to canter about without getting cornered. The returning herd discovered a rather magnificent new pony in their midst and there was some posturing and prancing – but they were soon preoccupied with grazing.

Working his way into the herd

Later, when the merged herds could migrate in and out of the barn together, it was interesting how the other ponies often tried to insist that D'Artagnan wait before allowing him to feed at the Haylage Bar. He nevertheless insisted on being amongst them, resisting their attempts to push him away. It seems to be a real necessity for a newcomer to insist on being 'in the herd'. If they can be easily

Feeding the big herd – everyone finds a place.

Returning to the home paddocks for the winter.

101

Above left to right:

Holtball Kick-em Jenny and her daughter Princess Cristal;

D'Artagnan with Holtball Baluran and Topaz;

Harry makes it clear to D'Artagnan his position in the herd.

pushed away, the herd gives them little status, and they are more likely to be bullied. While D'Artagnan recognised that he couldn't be a leader, he was certainly determined to 'belong'. This shimmying and shuffling into their midst was an important route to acceptance. Of course, in the wild, if a pony can't get accepted into a herd, he or she is at more risk of being attacked by predators if they are on the outskirts, or worse, on their own. So achieving acceptance is part of their survival instinct. D'Artagnan nevertheless had his work cut out as within a large herd like this are many different relationships, personalities and moods, as well as a constantly shifting hierarchy.

Harry 'supervising' D'Artagnan in the barn.

Tom Faggus meets the barefoot trimmer

When our barefoot trimmer Clive Ponsford visited, I very much hoped that Tom Faggus would now accept having his feet rasped. With the help of an enticing bowl of feed and a very careful Clive, Tom did indeed have his feet rasped for the first time and I was very pleased with him. His polite demeanour made the painstakingly effort to socialise him completely worthwhile. Tom had taught me about patience, tolerance, suppression of my own ego – and to allow him the time it takes for him to find the confidence and build the necessary trust to accept handling. He had also learned to suppress his natural tendency to be defensive as a first response. While Tom wasn't yet jumping through hoops, we had nevertheless taken some big steps forward.

Making time for individuals in an even larger herd

Wild-born Exmoor ponies need time, patience, kindness and understanding to evolve into the kind of ponies suitable for the more conventional equestrian performance activities. Once they trust people, they are the most fantastic ponies – intelligent, strong, agile, quick-thinking, highly trainable and they'll look after you. But like all relationships, it needs working at. The ponies need regular individual attention

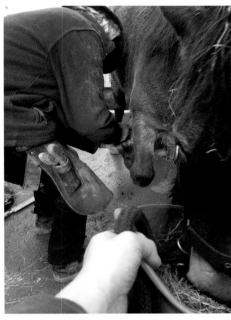

Tom Faggus is finally ready to accept having his feet trimmed by Clive Ponsford.

Spending time with the big herd – here with Lady Martha lying down.

to continue building their trust and confidence and often working alone, this was sometimes not easy for me to achieve. Their numbers had increased because we had given various ponies a lifeline and looking at the immense quality of the ponies we'd helped, I had no regrets. This was a challenge and process that just had to be worked out and worked through. It was, however, rather a daunting prospect and I wondered how on earth I was going to do it as we headed into the winter routine.

As I was coming to greatly appreciate, it was once again the herd that showed me the way. Arriving at the barn where the ponies had migrated in for some hay and a rest, I was feeling a little perplexed at where to start. One of the ponies, Imperial Topaz, stepped forward and came up to me for a fuss. I scratched his neck and we made a lovely connection. Then Scarlet came alongside and also had some attention. Some of the ponies carried on what they were doing and others watched our interactions with interest. There appeared to be some kind of equine 'queue' forming within the herd – where ponies would wait, and then approach me. I was able to move around and meet, greet, do a little grooming, check them over, spend some time, and then move on. Some of the ponies did not want to approach, and sometimes there were flurries of disagreement between them, or one pony would feel another had had enough attention and make their feelings about that clear. While my natural human tendency was to organise the ponies and conduct structured 'sessions' according to my criteria, the ponies were showing me how it was possible to offer them individual attention and achieve valuable interactions, within the herd environment. To engage with them like this, I had to relinquish my inclination to go out there with a 'plan' and instead, go with an attitude and openness to see what unfolded.

Each time I visited the herd, there were differences in how the ponies approached me and some that had not approached the day before would now seek me out. It was an opportunity for me to observe them more carefully and read them more deeply.

When I stopped worrying about how to give them individual attention, and started listening to the herd and taking what the ponies offered me – the information they revealed was fascinating. Some of the ponies are fond of standing expectantly on the podium or bridge, on their own or as a small group. This kind of gesture is often offered from a shyer and more introverted pony who is keen to interact and be noticed – but not necessarily feeling confident or inclined to directly approach me and 'compete' with the more extrovert ponies. I'm always careful to reward these 'tries'. Tuning into their herd energy is an amazing learning experience and slowly but surely, the ponies are showing me that what can appear to be overwhelming in terms of dealing with the sheer number of them, can actually become proactive and progressive group learning sessions – with a distinct and clear two-way exchange of information.

I used this special time among them to groom, check feet, slip head collars on and off, practice some drawing to me, feet-moving and playing with some of the agility challenges. Or simply sitting with them when they're lying down and resting. I always come away from these herd group sessions with new knowledge and understanding and feeling enriched with the positive energy that radiates from the herd.

Monsieur Chapeau loves to stand on the podium and bridge.

Opposite, top left: Ponies who wanted to interact would often stand on the bridge or podium and seek attention – here Topaz, Princess Khaleesi and Dazzler.

Top right: Prince Kailash and Princess Khaleesi.

Bottom: Nick and Dawn with the herd.

Chapter Fourteen
A Welcome Surprise

A mystery is solved as the moor yields some elusive ponies

December was soon upon us and I remained perplexed as to the whereabouts of Foxglove and her foal. The Floyd family arranged to gather in their magnificent Tippbarlake herd from Brendon Common and included a sweep of the adjacent Buscombe moorland to ensure that all the ponies were brought in. This included the mare and colt foal who had been let back out onto the moor from the Farleywater gathering.

When the Floyd family were sorting out ponies back at the farm, the paint marks on the mare and foal were noticed and, after further investigation, the mare was finally identified as Foxglove and it was remarked that the colt looked like a 'Bear foal'. The South family collected both the mare and foal and, as you can imagine, we headed straight over to Farleywater Farm to see them. As the colt and his mother emerged into the yard, I felt the hairs on the back of my neck tingle. He certainly had the stamp and presence of his father Bear. Of course, it could only be DNA testing that would prove his parentage, but we were all were pretty sure this time that the sire was Bear.

We arranged for Foxglove to accompany her colt to our farm so he could also benefit from a gradual weaning. We hadn't anticipated taking two moorland colt foals this year, but sometimes, that's the way it works out.

Back at the farm, it was lovely to see Foxglove greeting her fellow herd companion, Lark, and the new colt greeting Sitka – they had of course grown up together out on the moor. Our own mares, Penelope Pitstop and Maisie, along with their sons Pierre Parfait and Kilimanjaro, looked on with a mixture of suspicion and anticipation at the newcomers. That first afternoon, there were two distinct little 'herds' in the field – the Farleywater ponies and our Herd 11 ponies.

What to name the new colt?
The new colt needed a name. Sitting in the kitchen with Millie Ker we discussed various names but nothing seemed to be right. Then Millie laughingly suggested 'Yogi Bear' and we all looked at each other. The colt was strong, fluffy, with the most beautiful blond highlights in his mane and big, captivating eyes.

'That's it. Yogi Bear is perfect,' I said. And Nick agreed.

'Let's hope he's definitely a Bear son with a name like that.'

So Yogi Bear it was.

The 'real' Foxglove and her colt foal.

The colt looked very much like he'd been sired by Bear.

Pierre Parfait and Yogi Bear

Pierre Parfait is smaller and younger than Yogi Bear, but he was determined to be the boss of the new arrival. This was conveyed pretty rudely. Yogi Bear was initially very shy of coming into the barn and everything had to be completely quiet and safe before he'd make his way in and start to tentatively eat haylage out of a tyre. At this point, Pierre would often purposefully manoeuvre himself backwards to shunt Yogi Bear out of the way. It was interesting to see that the colt didn't respond with aggression, but nor did he behave like a subordinate and shy away. Instead, he tolerated Pierre Parfait's behaviour, absorbing as much of the shunting as he could and maintaining an unconcerned appearance. The early signs of leadership. Pierre Parfait may have thought he was asserting himself over Yogi Bear but I cautioned him:

'I'd be careful Pierre Parfait, because I think you may be storing up trouble for yourself.'

Pierre may well have been mirroring his mother's behaviour, because Penelope Pitstop tried the same kind of behaviour with Foxglove. As the youngest mare, Penelope had received short thrift from the older mares, Lark and Maisie – who both conveyed in the most disdainful manner (I'm thinking 'Dame Maggie' here) that she was bottom of the pecking order. She did not like this and was extremely keen to have someone beneath her. This privilege was awarded to the newcomer, Foxglove. However, Foxglove was also older, wiser and more experienced than Penelope and, like her son, I saw her avoid confrontation and tolerate Penelope's fairly outrageous attempts to bully her without returning aggression or escalating the situation. Although able to move Foxglove away, Penelope was

Yogi Bear and Foxglove are reunited with Lark and Sitka and meet Maisie, Penelope Pitstop, Pierre Parfait and Kilimanjaro

not gaining respect among the mares with her rather petulant behaviour. This environment was a wonderful learning opportunity for young Penelope, on many levels, and all part of growing up.

It did occur to me, watching all of this, that we humans can learn a thing or two from the ponies with regard to dealing with bullies!

Taking a DNA sample from the rather wild Yogi Bear

With Christmas looming, there was a pressing need for the vet to visit and microchip Yogi Bear, along with completing a passport form ('silhouette') and taking a DNA sample from his mane or tail so his parentage could be verified. This all had to be done before the end of the year. The vet was booked but I came down with a bout of flu, so we had to postpone, and by the time I was well enough, there was only time for a few short socialisation sessions.

Yogi Bear was reminiscent of Bear as a foal, remaining highly sensitised to people and preferring to stay behind the other ponies whenever we appeared. Nevertheless, he had thankfully not been plastered in horrible hot brands like his father, so while wary, he was not dangerously explosive like Bear had been. While Sitka's mother Lark had quickly decided that we were friends, Yogi's mother Foxglove remained wary and her son followed her lead. Although they were tentatively starting to remain in the barn when we appeared, they would soon both make a rapid exit whenever we moved around doing the chores, however carefully we went about it.

Above left to right:

The band of four colts spend hours playing together.

Pierre Parfait and Kilimanjaro.

Below, left to right:

Sitka and Pierre Parfait play fighting.

The beautiful Farleywater Foxglove.

Pierre Parfait playing with Kilimanjaro.

I could see that getting Yogi Bear to willingly accept a head collar was going to take time – and we didn't have it before the vet visit. But I didn't want him 'grabbed and restrained' to have the microchip inserted, nor have a head collar forced on – so my plan was to see if I could get him to willingly accept standing in the handling shute, where the microchip could be inserted calmly and without any hands-on restraint. However, as Yogi Bear was so wary of standing in the barn with us, he first had to learn to cope with standing in a 15ft x 15ft pen without panicking – let alone the shute.

Foxglove and Yogi Bear were relatively easy to gently herd into the pen and rather than shut them in, I let them discover that they could leave it through the shute. When they were used to this, I started closing the door to the pen and giving them a feed, so there was a pleasant association with the experience.

Although the vet's visit was looming, I knew that building Yogi Bear's confidence of standing in a smaller area was vital. He could now stand in the pen on his own and let me join him – and he was learning, through the use of a gentle advance and retreat approach, to tentatively step towards me and touch a feather duster with his nose. He discovered that he could 'stop' me approaching by giving me his attention, which helped him become more comfortable about positively engaging with me – but he remained very wary.

This stage of socialisation takes the time it takes – yet we needed to progress to actual body contact in order for him to let a stranger insert a microchip and examine him at close quarters, in a few short days.

This initial patience paid off because Yogi soon accepted standing in the shute with me quietly closing the gates at each end so he was contained inside, and he let me stroke his rump. His ability to think, process and lower his adrenaline indicated a sensitive and trainable temperament. During this short session, Foxglove watched intently but calmly and her steady expression told me that she realised I did not mean Yogi Bear any harm. An understanding was established between us.

I let Yogi out to re-join his mother and from this day they were both more accepting of our presence in the barn when we skipped out and replenished the hay tyres. Over the next few days Yogi Bear progressed to letting me gently stroke him all along his body and up his neck. I say 'cope' because this is what it was. We still had a long way to go before he fully relaxed.

The vet meets Yogi Bear

When the vet arrived, he first had to microchip and take DNA samples from Bear's sons Pierre Parfait and Kilimanjaro, who accepted this while standing in the pen with their mothers, wearing head collars and on lead ropes. It's not a comfortable experience, but they both coped well and I couldn't have asked for more from them.

Then it was time for Yogi to go into the pen and shute. The vet approached him very quietly and carefully and I'm proud to say that the brave little colt foal accepted the microchip and hair sample being taken, without any panic. He trusted me that nothing terrible was going to happen to him. The DNA sample was sent off to the breed society.

Yogi Bear finds the confidence to tentatively start to interact with the feather duster.

Making the muzzle to hand greeting and first touch.

Opposite, clockwise
from top left:
Lark has relaxed well into her winter off the moor;
Pierre Parfait;
Pierre Parfait trying to 'boss' Yogi Bear;
Yogi Bear with his mother Foxglove in their winter coats;
a meeting of foals – Yogi Bear, Pierre Parfait and Sitka;
Handsome Yogi Bear.

Bear is indeed the sire
of Yogi Bear.

Right: Yogi Bear.

Over the winter, training time was scarce and I had to prioritise working with the ponies who needed to have a physical inspection to enter the Exmoor Pony Society Stud Book. While Sitka had already passed his inspection at the Farleywater gathering, Yogi Bear, Pierre Parfait and Kilimanjaro had not yet been seen. There were also three other ponies at the farm who needed an inspection – Tom Faggus, Lady Myrtleberry of Countisbury and Holtball Princess Cristal.

The DNA results arrive
We eventually received the welcome news that Yogi Bear was indeed the son of Bear. Now all that remained was for him to pass the physical inspection that would allow him to become a pedigree registered Exmoor pony.

Nearly there but not quite – DNA cannot help Lady Martha, or can it?
Some weeks after we had received the DNA results for Yogi Bear, the DNA testing of Lady Martha of Molland Moor confirmed that her father is indeed one of the two licensed stallions who had escaped onto Molland Moor. However, her mother is not one of the very few remaining pedigree-registered mares in Herd 99 – which means that Lady Martha is a daughter of one of their descendants. But these descendants, having not been inspected and registered as foals – and then going on to breed

Molland Moor siblings, Lady
Martha and Lady Molly.

themselves – cannot be entered into the stud book, because there is no supplement and upgrading system within it to embrace 'missed out' ponies. With a pedigree sire (who is now sadly dead) Lady Martha is a prime candidate for DNA 'purity' testing – which we hope will be facilitated following the completion of the Exmoor Pony DNA Whole Genome Project that I mentioned earlier.

This project is a collaboration of Exmoor National Park Authority, the Moorland Exmoor Pony Breeders Group (including the Molland Estate and Badgworthy Land Company), Rare Breeds Survival Trust, Exmoor Pony Society and vet Peter Green, chaired by DEFRA Chief Vet and RBST Trustee, Tim Morris. The group is working with Dr Sarah Blott at Nottingham University and is in the process of sampling a carefully selected number of genetically highly-representative Exmoor ponies. The 'whole genome' of these ponies will be mapped through sequencing, followed by genotyping of a further, wider sample base. The results will form a 'cluster' that will define the 'Exmoor Pony' – and be representative of as much range and diversity within the breed as possible. It is hoped that this will facilitate a genetic 'baseline' against which any Exmoor pony can be cost-effectively DNA tested to determine purity – so ponies whose genetic profiles fall inside the 'cluster' will be deemed to be purebred.

I sit on the project team and we hope that this new research will provide the basis for embracing and recognising Exmoor ponies like Lady Martha who are currently being excluded – and lost – from the breeding gene pool. Perhaps science is finally finding a way to safeguard the Exmoor pony genetics that we are currently losing – on Exmoor, across the UK and worldwide? I hope so.

So Lady Martha, the tiny little late-born foal, who showed such presence and self-possession at her herd's gathering – along with her older sibling Lady Molly and other Molland Moor mares and ponies like Holtball Black Bess (granddaughter of Herd 23's The Highwayman) – may well hold the key to making a useful contribution to the Exmoor pony breed in the future.

Moorland Tom – one of the unregisterable Molland Moor colts.

Below left: The unregistered Molland Moor Exmoor ponies.

Below right: Holtball Black Bess.

Chapter Fifteen

Saving a Moorland Herd

Herd 423, with the very last foals sired by Bear's father, finds itself in jeopardy

Bear's magnificent father, Great Gatsby, sadly died in early 2016. He had been running with James Bryant's Herd 423 on Countisbury – a challenging moorland area surrounding Kipscombe Farm, which spans the busy A39 road and across to the dramatic Countisbury cliffs and Foreland lighthouse. Here, the ponies require considerable stamina and must keep their wits about them to survive and thrive in this exposed and sometimes perilous environment. With Great Gatsby gone, the foals of 2016 were his very last progeny.

During the summer, James informed us that he was sadly going to leave his farm, which is owned by the National Trust, and the future of his herd was something of a concern. James was not able to take the ponies with him and he felt that, after years of getting them established and leared in their current environment, it would ideally be best if at least a core herd could remain on Countisbury. However, even if this could be arranged, it would likely involve only the mares, with perhaps one mature stallion – and James also had various other stallions and colts, as well as all of the 2016 foals. They now faced a very uncertain future.

Exmoor pony enthusiast, Christina Verfurth, offered two young stallions, Fitz and Goblin, a home with her in Germany.

James had a number of lovely two-year-old colts, but he had been told that it would be 'difficult' to confirm their parentage and register them – and he made the reluctant decision to euthanise them. When he broke the news to me about the colts, I was sad – and not a little frustrated – and resolved to try and do everything I could to help him safeguard the rest of the ponies and particularly the foals. One issue to tackle was why James was being told it would be 'difficult' to register his ponies and we were determined to get to the bottom of this.

With James flat out busy trying to deal with the logistics of a complete farm move and building work at his new home, along with his young family, Christmas came and went before an inspection of his foals could be organised. Time was running out because the foals could not realistically be advertised for sale until they were pedigree registered and had passports. The inspection was eventually organised for early February – with James's leaving date looming at the end of the month.

The question remained about the future of the herd. James had discussions with the National

One of Great Gatsby's very last foals.

Opposite: Bear's father Great Gatsby running with the Countisbury Herd 423 mares.

The Bryant family children – Alice, Poppy and Oscar with Jack just out of the picture.

Bringing the foals through the shute to microchip them.

Mare and foal reunited.

Trust and it was thankfully agreed that they would purchase the herd, enabling the ponies to remain in their home environment of Kipscombe. The grazing restrictions meant that this could not include any of the 2016 foals. So homes would have to be found for them all in the few short weeks we had left. We could not fail.

To ease the process of identifying and registering the foals, two days before their inspection I spent a day with James and his family to sort out the herd. Assisted by James' partner Roz and their children Jack, Oscar, Alice and Poppy – we would compile a list of all the ponies and get the foals microchipped by the vet, who would also take DNA samples for parentage testing. The plan was to run the foals (or technically yearlings now) through the handling shute for the vet.

I noticed a little dark-coloured filly in a separate pen from the other foals and when I asked after her, I was told she wouldn't be put forward for inspection as she was 'smaller and darker' than the others. The little filly stared intently at me, blissfully unaware of the predicament she was in. I pointed out that many people adore the 'smaller and darker' Exmoors and I wondered how I could persuade James to include the filly in the group to be inspected.

During this time, most of the semi-feral mares stayed well away from the pens, either on the outskirts of the yard area or in the adjoining field. But one mare came closer, braving everyone and trotting over to stand directly outside the pens and stare into the barn – whickering deeply to the foals inside. She was a lovely strong, dark mare and it was easy to spot that it was the dear little dark filly who was her daughter. The filly whinnied back to her mother. There was clearly an immense bond between them and it tugged at my heart strings – as I believe it was meant to. This mare was determined to help her foal.

The other youngsters came through the shute, in pairs or on their own, to be microchipped, have their passport silhouettes completed and DNA samples taken. As they were not experiencing actual physical restraint and no-one was inside the shute with them, they coped well with the experience and allowed the vet to insert their microchips. Each foal was sprayed with a bright paint mark number for visual identification. After the vet had finished with each pony, they were let out to the field, where they cantered off to join their mothers.

When the last one had been through, a decision had still not been made regarding the little dark filly – and the vet left. There, standing in the pen was the filly, with her mother waiting anxiously outside for her foal. Not being known as someone who easily gives up, I brought the discussion around to her once again and said I was pretty sure I could find a buyer for such an endearing character. To my relief, it was decided to let her rejoin her mother and put her forward for the inspection after all. She hadn't been microchipped or had a passport silhouette completed yet, but we were one step further towards securing her future. As mother and foal trotted off to the field, I could see their sides bumping against each other. They were so close – I felt a lump in my throat and resolved that whatever happened, I would secure The Chocolate Teddy Bear, as I'd nicknamed her, a good home.

That day, we also paired up each mare with their foal and the identity of each mare was checked against the passports and recorded on a list, together with the microchip numbers and details of the

Above left: Mares and foals being turned out again.

The Chocolate Teddy Bear and her mother Flower.

foals seen that morning. Often, we found it difficult and even impossible to decipher the branded marks on the mares, even when they were clipped out. Some of them were microchipped and some were not. Once they were identified, they were also sprayed with a paint mark number, so there would be no confusion at the inspection. On inspection day, all of the foals passed, including The Chocolate Teddy Bear filly, whose DNA was taken and silhouette completed. She just needed a microchip which James would arrange. It was now a question of waiting for the DNA results so the pedigree registrations could be completed and passports issued. Although DNA testing can take some weeks or even months sometimes, we hoped that the preliminary work we had done to correctly identify and match the mares with the foals would make it straightforward – not 'difficult'. With not even three weeks remaining until James vacated his farm, the pressure was now on to find some new owners.

Help from Marc and Martin from Germany

As luck would have it, at this very time, German wild horse film-maker, Marc Lubetzki and global wildlife photographer, Martin Buschmann, were photographing and filming the free-living Exmoor ponies. Exmoor pony owner and enthusiast in Germany, Nadine Vollmar, put them in touch with us and we arranged a meeting to find out more about their work. After hearing of the plight of the Herd 423 foals, they offered to help us by making a short film promoting the foals and taking some photographs.

James Bryant had the herd running in a group of fields on the farm. When we arrived, Martin went off to take some moorland pictures and Marc and I approached the mares and foals and sat quietly in their midst. They viewed us with interest and curiosity. One little filly, Ivy, tentatively made her way over and reached out to make a connection with me – allowing us to get some beautiful pictures of her. Touchingly, The Chocolate Teddy Bear filly remained lying down while I photographed her. The intensity of her connection is reflected in the pictures. The enchanting way the foals responded to us

Dawn and Nick with Marc Lubetzki.

From top: Dawn connecting with filly foal, Ivy;
The Chocolate Teddy Bear;
Filly foal Imogen.

Right: The ponies make good use of the whole terrain, grazing the top of this stone-ditched bank.

that afternoon was a moving experience. They were all beautiful foals — engaging, sentient creatures who deserved to find good homes.

The following day, Marc and I sat in the kitchen at Holt Ball creating the short film. This, together with the photographs, duly went out on social media, receiving thousands of views. We were soon receiving enquiries to pass to James Bryant. Slowly but surely people started reserving the foals and one of the first foals reserved was The Chocolate Teddy Bear — to Jackie Sparrow, who helps many ponies through her Second Chance Equine project. Christine Verfurth chose the colt Iggy Pop to travel to Germany, and filly, Isobella, was selected to run with the Porlock 100 herd, arranged with herd owner Matthew Coldicutt. Sam Saunders in Devon chose two fillies, Ice Ice Baby and Ivanka; Sarah Fletcher from Cornwall chose Imogen; and Susannah and Yakob Darling Khan chose colts Ivor and Ivanhoe. Walter Albert from Ireland chose Icarus and Ivy and Gillian Stewart, also from Ireland, chose Izzy and Idris.

The deadline for James to move out of his farm was now almost upon us and with pending DNA parentage verification, the foals needed basic identification passports to travel. These were collected by Nick Westcott — in the nick of time — on the very morning we needed to deliver four of the foals to their new homes in Devon and the day before the transporter arrived to collect the foals going to Ireland. Over the coming weeks, the remaining foals safely reached their destinations.

On the day James and his family moved out of the farm, I helped him with the transfer of his mare herd to the National Trust and each pony was identified and ticked off against the list. It all went smoothly until one young mare came through the pens, who didn't appear to be microchipped, nor could her individual pony brand be deciphered. She was separated from the others as only fully identified mares could be accepted during the handover. It also became evident that the mature stallion, Helmantor Hannibal, would not after all be joining the herd transfer. This left both ponies in somewhat of a predicament — with James leaving his farm by midnight that very evening. He agreed

to take the mare and stallion and accommodate them at his new property for a short period, while I tried to find homes for them. Thankfully, after some promotion on social media, Natalie Rose agreed to take Helmantor Hannibal into her re-wilding project at Rosewood Farm in Yorkshire, to run with her Exmoor pony mares. Jackie Sparrow agreed to take the mystery mare, along with The Chocolate Teddy Bear — and they were both given a wonderful opportunity to undertake their initial socialisation with Ian Vandenburgh.

When the DNA results arrived, all of the foals had been correctly parentage verified to their dams and all had been sired by Great Gatsby — except one. The dear little Chocolate Teddy Bear's sire was a mystery, so testing continued against other possible stallions. It turned out that Helmantor Hannibal had sired 'Teddy' and Jackie was now the owner of one of his precious few daughters.

Everyone was pleased with their new ponies and we breathed a huge sigh of relief. All of the mares had been safeguarded and the precious last progeny of Great Gatsby — Bear's half brothers and sisters — had found good homes, along with the Herd 423 stallions. Herd 423 will continue to run on the moors at Countisbury under the stewardship of the North Devon National Trust, as the Foreland Herd. It had taken some organisation and effort to register and find homes for the foals — but identifying them had not been difficult at all.

From top: MEPBG Exmoor Pony Show 2016 foal champion Isobella is staying on the moor;

colt Iggy Pop;

filly Ivanka.

Chapter Sixteen

A Complete Surprise!

After months of waiting there is a fantastic discovery

Back at the Farleywater gathering in October, when Yogi Bear and his mother had been let back out onto the moor, it was thought that the young mare Narcissa had not had a foal. I'd been surprised about that, as Bear's close bond with her was evident – something I'd been sure would result in a foal. But that hadn't apparently been the case. After the gathering, some of the foals had remained at Farleywater Farm over the winter, while DNA testing to confirm their parentage continued. Eventually, as spring approached, it was discovered that one colt, Navajo, was sired by stallion Wortleberry but he was out of a Tippbarlake herd mare. He was returned to the Floyd family and has now found a lovely new home with Charlie Pearce. Then, the mother of a beautiful filly called Cherokee was identified as being Narcissa – and Bear was confirmed as the sire. This was the best possible news – the two lovebirds had produced a foal after all! It was decided that Cherokee will remain in the South family's Farleywater herd. With four pedigree registered progeny, Yogi Bear, Tanana, Kenai and now Cherokee, who will live on the moor, it had been a very successful breeding programme for Bear.

Left and above: The beautiful filly Farleywater Cherokee.

Top: Bear and his special mare Narcissa did have a foal after all.

Opposite: Bear's daughter, Farleywater Cherokee.

121

Holtball Herd 11 foundation mare Maisie (Smarty Pants) and Holtball Kilimanjaro.

Chapter Seventeen
Weaning the Colts

As time approaches for the mares to leave, there's an unexpected development!

Lambing was now upon us at Holt Ball and sleep became a snatched luxury. This time of year can pass in a blur with almost round-the-clock work, so pony handling sessions were short through necessity rather than desire. It was also time to start gradually weaning the colts from their mothers. While the moorbred colts had been born as early as last April, Kilimanjaro had arrived late (mid-August), so it was important for him to remain with his mother for as long as possible.

Mature moorland brood mares can have a naturally rotund appearance. However, Yogi Bear's dam Foxglove was starting to look not so much 'well' from over-wintering on the farm, but that she was potentially in foal. This had not been expected, but doing the calculations, it was just possible that, if Bear had got her in foal as soon as he'd arrived at Farleywater and she'd foaled in early April, then Wortleberry might just have been able to cover her on her foal heat (about ten days after foaling) before he had been removed from the moor. It was a fine margin, but definitely possible, so we monitored Foxglove closely. Unlike the other mares, she had started to naturally wean Yogi Bear and while he still spent time with his mother, she was discouraging him from suckling – another sign that she may be conserving her energy for a new foal.

To begin the process of weaning, I created a taped-off route from one pasture to another and drifted Lark, Foxglove and Penelope at liberty, away from the colts to the new pasture. At first, they only spent an hour or two there, before returning to their sons. I repeated this each day, slightly extending the time they spent away. Initially, as Kilimanjaro was so much younger, I left his mother Maisie with him and only separated the three other mares. Although it was time-consuming, it enabled the mares and colts to gradually get used to being separated. By the time Maisie joined the mares each day, Kilimanjaro had got accustomed to being in the 'colt band' for part of the day and was better able to accept the separation from his mother. At first, there was various calling from both groups, while the mares also appreciated some different grass in the new pasture. This gradually reduced as everyone got used to the new routine. While the mares were away, I was able to progress interaction sessions with the colts and give them a feed – a positive association with the separation time.

Yogi Bear was still very 'nose sensitive' – keen to engage but head shy – so I introduced a silky scarf and encouraged him to put his nose through a loop of the soft material – and this progressed to him

Top: Foxglove looking increasingly 'large' with Yogi Bear.

Above: It was time to wean the mares from their colt foals.

The colts grazed in a tight band when getting used to separation from their dams.

From top: Yogi Bear learning to accept a head collar; one of their last days with their mothers; Kilimanjaro, Yogi Bear and Pierre Parfait.

accepting wearing a head collar. He learned quickly and his ability to work out what to do was impressive. He was now tentatively allowing me to groom him and also starting to let me brush down his legs and ask for a foot. It was essential that he could willingly offer his feet before we could arrange an inspection. With five other ponies also waiting for their inspection, I was keen for Yogi to progress, so we could set a date.

The mares and colts became increasingly comfortable with being separated and were starting to spend whole nights and part of the day apart. Despite being in foal, Foxglove was still keen to return to Yogi Bear with the other mares. He now accepted that he was not allowed to suckle her and was happy to stand beside her. The bond between them was very strong and Foxglove often took Yogi away from the group and stood over him while he was lying down. It was as if she was preparing him to continue his life without her.

Hellos and goodbyes

It was just at the point when I was thinking about completing the weaning, when circumstances at the farm meant that one night, the mares remained with their sons overnight. The next morning, Nick called me to say, 'Go and have a look in the colt field.' And there was Foxglove with a brand new foal. The rest of the herd was relaxed and grazing and Yogi Bear was standing quietly nearby. He had seen his mother give birth to his half brother and would now be better able to understand why she needed to leave him. The colts followed me in for a feed and I quietly separated the mares and took them, along with Foxglove and her new foal, to the other pasture. The colts could still see their mothers when they came up into the corral, so they knew where they were. The weaning was now complete.

This was no bad thing as, despite supplementary feeding, we'd noticed that Kilimanjaro's mother, Maisie, was losing condition. This was extremely unlike Maisie and I hoped that, now weaned from her foal, she could recover her usual form.

Foxglove's foal finding his feet!

The colts soon settled into a tight band – grazing together and migrating into the barn and lying down together. With their mothers now permanently separated, I had the opportunity to build a stronger bond with them. Foxglove's new son was doing well and once he was strong enough to travel, the plan was to return them, along with Lark, to the moor, where he could experience living wild and free out on Buscombe with other foals. Although it would be possible for the mares to run with stallion Bear before returning to the moor, we and their owners felt that they should both have a breeding rest.

A special friendship

It has been a privilege hosting these two wild mares for the winter and an incredible opportunity to learn from them, as they let us into their world. I had not expected that it would be possible to form such a strong, cognitive bond with completely unsocialised, mature, wild-born mares – working with them and their sons in close proximity and requiring them to sometimes navigate and manoeuvre within small areas. Also, calling them to come to me from the pasture, and drifting them across to new pastures and back again. They have been nothing short of amazing – and a joy to work with. While I've made a deliberate effort not to 'tame' them and accepted what they wanted to offer me, I've been deeply moved by the very conscious friendship and trust bestowed on me by nineteen-year-old Lark, the mother of Sitka.

When she came to Holt Ball to help her son make the transition to life off the moors, it would have been understandable if she'd remained wild-natured and suspicious of us and the farm's environment, with its barns and contained areas. Yet from the moment she arrived, she immediately grasped that we had good intentions and she showed a desire to connect. While she can robustly square up to other mares, she has always been extremely careful to move around me gently and politely. She and I have become firm friends and she seeks me out and allows me, and others, to stroke her. Her behaviour and energy indicate a mare who is appreciative and enjoying her time with us. She is a very special, wise old mare who has allowed me further into the secretive world of the wild-born ponies. A great privilege indeed.

A very special friendship had developed with Lark.

Chapter Eighteen

A Huge Step Forward

A decision is made which brings great welfare improvement for Exmoor ponies

As we have seen with Herd 23, some herd owners are now keeping foals who have failed inspection for having paler colouration on their sole plates, but are otherwise quality ponies. They do not want to lose these animals from their breeding programmes – particularly when they represent the rare dun/golden-redder bay colourings. There are also increasing concerns regarding the health and safety aspects of restraining wild-born foals and youngstock at the inspections and forcing their feet up to look at the sole plates – which is often their first experience of handling. This can result in explosive reactions, risking injury to both handlers and ponies, and can cause the ponies stress.

As I've mentioned, the MEPBG had made requests to the breed society to discontinue picking up the feet of foals during inspections. A vote was put to the membership at the 2017 Exmoor Pony Society AGM and they agreed to stop picking up the feet with immediate effect – initiating one of the most significant welfare improvements for the Exmoor pony breed since the reduction in hot branding (2012 and 2014 Ref: DEFRA Code of Practise for the Identification of Semi-feral Ponies). What remains uncertain is how ponies who have previously 'failed' inspection for this reason can be upgraded retrospectively and given pedigree status in the stud book – and discussions continue about this.

The rule change will now give owners the opportunity to gradually introduce their foals to the idea of willingly offering their feet, taking the time it takes. This can make the difference between a fearful or resentful pony who has learned to defensively kick out, and one where the thought of kicking his handler does not even enter his head.

Handsome Imperial Topaz waits to be upgraded to pedigree status, having only 'failed' inspection for two small pale patches underneath one foot.

Opposite: One of the most significant welfare improvements for the Exmoor pony breed in recent times.

The colts were becoming
strong and 'colty'.

Chapter Nineteen
The 'Uncles' Meet the Colts

The newly weaned colts receive some timely guidance and reassurance

Settling well after being weaned, the four colts were happy enough but also becoming rather boisterous and 'colty' and keen to test the boundaries with me. It was definitely time to introduce them to 'The Uncles'. I've found that some guidance from older ponies at this stage can be enormously helpful for youngsters. The elders are adept at teaching precocious colts what is and isn't appropriate behaviour, and once well acquainted, also provide some comfort and reassurance for the inevitable insecurities of yearlings who find themselves on their own after weaning.

Monsieur Chapeau was, of course, a natural choice for this job and while I was standing in the barn pondering who else to bring along, Otis stepped forward and made it clear that whatever was going on, he wanted to be part of it. Literally poking his nose through the head collar, he seemed to be saying, 'Come on, let's go and do this.'

We took them over to the colt field and there were some dramatic greetings. Sitka, the largest colt, immediately started trying to mount Monsieur Chapeau who, to his credit, dissuaded him assertively rather than aggressively. Sitka tried the same on Uncle Otis, who was more forthright in his rebuff and set off galloping around the pasture with Sitka galloping after him, for a number of impressive circuits. Otis has a magnificent thundering gallop, rather like an ancient Destrier, and the dry ground literally drummed. After this, some kind of understanding appeared to have been reached because Sitka reverted to making the submissive foaling gesture (snapping his jaws open and shut) to the older geldings, like the other colts.

It's fascinating to watch the interactions – with the older geldings delivering dramatic 'biting gestures', but in the most gentle way. Like pretending to bite at the colt's windpipe as if to say, 'I could kill you now, but I'm not going to – just be aware that I am the boss of you.' There is also nipping at hamstrings and much circling around, until the colts drop to their knees. The older geldings display 'fight' body language, making gestures like striking out and squealing, without actually making contact. Most of the drama in this first session took place with Sitka, who was the main 'challenger' to the arrival of the Uncles. The other three colts watched closely and tried to stay out of trouble.

Later, I decided to also add Uncle Harry to the group and the three geldings have brought some

Top: Full of energy – Yogi Bear and Kilimanjaro.

Sitka meets Monsieur Chapeau.

order and stability to the colt band. Sitka can now often be spotted politely mutually grooming with Uncle Otis and an equilibrium has been reached which is helping the colts' development enormously. It's making my job easier and once again, it is a herd environment that is providing the solutions.

Evolving attitudes with other owners

Alongside our own efforts to better understand and work with Exmoor ponies, there are also encouraging reports from the new owners. A welcome trend is people endeavouring to take a more considerate, patient and kind approach with their wild-born Exmoor ponies – and appreciating the huge step it must be for these spirited youngsters to adjust from living wild and free to a domestic environment. In just a few years, I've witnessed an increasing change in attitude, moving away from 'force and coercion' (ie, confinement, 'swinging' to halter break, roping, restraining, forcing on head collars and leaving ropes trailing, intimidation and beating, etc), to an opening of hearts and minds and a desire to properly and respectfully connect with the ponies. It's immensely heartening as more of these kind of people show an interest in Exmoor ponies and offer them good opportunities. The Exmoor breed needs this continued interest and evolution to survive and flourish.

Opposite page:
Otis leading Sitka on their gallop; Monsieur Chapeau and Yogi Bear; Otis meeting Sitka; Monsieur Chapeau with Pierre Parfait and Kilimanjaro; and bottom row, the colts interacting with the geldings.

Left: There is much cantering about as the Uncles get to know the colts.

Below: The newly formed herd is soon calm with the Uncles providing some welcome guidance as well as reassurance.
Monsieur Chapeau with Yogi Bear.

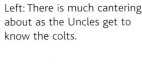

Other owners are developing wonderful relationships with their youngsters – Deborah Sheppard bonding with Jackie Sparrow's Chocolate Teddy Bear filly.

Right: Otis with his orderly group of young colts.

Opposite: It was time to say *Au revoir* to Lark, Foxglove and her colt foal as they returned to their moorland home of Buscombe to run with the rest of the Farleywater herd.

Lark, Foxglove and her colt foal return to the moor

With spring well under way the time arrived to bid farewell to Lark and Foxglove and her colt foal, and take them back to run wild and free on Buscombe. The foal was now mature enough to travel and they were all glowing with health. I have to confess that I've found it a wrench to part with Lark. I have learned so much from her and shall look out for her when the moor gets too much for an older lady, and see what can be done for her.

We padded the trailer floor with plenty of bedding and all three ponies loaded well and stood quietly inside. Nick drove them back to Buscombe and parked within sight of their herd. When he let down the ramp for them to unload, they cantered off joyfully to greet their herd members and introduce Foxglove's colt to his siblings. A perfect summer lies ahead for him as he lives in a wonderful expanse of moorland, until the autumn when the herd is gathered in. We will endeavour to help the South family find him a good home after weaning.

Lark

Chapter Twenty
The Call of the Herd

What the ponies are revealing – when we learn to listen

Through watching and listening to the ponies – both 'wild' and tame – and working to provide them with the company, environment, management systems and interactions that keep them happy – the ponies are continuing to open our eyes to what they ideally really need and want from us.

This contradicts some of the more conventional methods of keeping ponies that have become normal in past decades – like containing them in stables for long hours and only turning them out in small, sparse paddocks. This can be boring and lonely for intelligent, inquisitive ponies. They can munch through a small slice of hay and drink a bucket of water very quickly, leaving them with nothing to do but stare out of a stable (if they can see out) for hours on end. The lack of opportunity to properly migrate and graze/loaf/explore and play with companions – as they are designed to do – can result in mental, physical and metabolic problems, which can sometimes lead to weight gain, laminitis and even ulcers, along with stiff joints. Boredom and frustration can cause behavioural issues, and lack of company means the ponies can't engage in the normal social herd behaviour.

This can be further exacerbated by 'unnatural' clipping of their thick winter coats, metal shoeing and over-rugging, which can mean that the ponies can't easily regulate their bodies during the seasons, as nature intended. Add to that handling and training that involves punishment and demands obedience irrespective of feelings, and it's hardly surprising then, that some ponies may not feel like giving their best when asked to do the bidding of humans in ridden or other work. If their attempts to express their anxiety, frustration, discomfort and unhappiness fall on deaf ears or are not even noticed – they can internalise their emotions and 'shut down', sometimes resulting in being unfairly labelled 'difficult', naughty or stubborn.

It sounds obvious, but ponies are not 'baby horses' – and they deserve as much respect, kindness and consideration as their larger and perhaps more commanding relative – the horse. Even more so when they have lived wild and free in semi-feral family herds and experienced 'survival of the fittest', requiring independent thinking and making their own choices. The stimulation and education of a free-living environment is a world away from the lonely confinement of a small pony stable, where people may not consider what the ponies are really thinking and feeling – and only 'communicate' by telling, not asking. We can do so much more to improve and enrich the lives of ponies – and thankfully, more and more people are beginning to understand this.

From the left: Monty, Topaz and Scarlet.

Opposite: Dawn connecting with the herd.

135

With enhanced awareness from us, the ponies are more able and likely to offer us erudite interactions and responses.

We can learn to truly observe and see what is actually there – rather than what we want to see.

What's ideal and what's practical ...

There are of course practical considerations to keeping ponies in herds and moving towards a more natural and free-living management system. When they gleefully dive into a wallow in the depths of winter – plastering themselves in freezing mud to add insulation and protection against the cold and wind – it's obvious that this is not ideal for riding them! There's no doubt that clean, clipped, rugged, stable-kept ponies offer a far more convenient prospect for giving a quick brush over, tacking up and taking out or schooling. However, watching our herds migrating in and out from the pasture, able to move around extensively, seeking grazing, forage and company as they need it – and happily dealing with the elements with what nature has equipped them with – my feeling is that hairy, sometimes muddy ponies living in a sociable herd are more likely to be physically and mentally fulfilled, well-balanced – and happy. We prefer to see them like that and so we've adjusted our training and management of them accordingly. I feel we are reaping the rewards of better connection and understanding with the ponies as a result.

Aspects of this kind of larger herd management can be easily incorporated into 'mini-herds' of two or three ponies – with adaption of existing shelter and turnout areas to provide a more interesting, stimulating – and healthy – lifestyle. Creating walking routes and interesting loafing areas, different surfaces, water areas, and providing company and objects to play with, along with the opportunity to freely migrate within those areas, can make an enormous positive difference to the day to day lives of ponies, physically and mentally.

Reaching a compromise

Watching the free-living ponies out in their wonderful, challenging moorland environments – where they can make full use of their intelligence and enjoy true family herd life – is inspiring us to incorporate as many elements of that as we can into their lives off the moor. What we're doing here is all about compromise. Engaging with the ponies in a way that respects what they want too and endeavouring to establish two-way communication – rather than just making them do what we want, for our convenience. In return, they are opening up to us, showing us that they can take far more responsibility for themselves and each other than we originally thought. They're capable of understanding, learning, adapting and responding to what we ask of them – even at liberty and from a significant distance, as we've seen with the long-range herd recall.

Tuning into equine emotions

Horses and ponies experience a full range of emotions and when we open our hearts and minds to that, we can become more considerate of their feelings and what we ask of them. We can tune into our intuitive feelings and senses, quieten our egos, pause and listen, and become mindful and in the present moment. We can learn to truly observe – and see what is actually there, rather than what we want to see. We can be more receptive and give ponies the time they need to adjust and process what we want from them. With this open, grounded, enhanced awareness from us, the ponies are more able and likely to offer us erudite interactions and responses – on many levels – for the long term.

Top: There are practical considerations to allowing ponies to live naturally in herds as Monsieur Chapeau demonstrates here with his impressively muddy coat!

Above: Encouraging ponies to express how they feel to evolve willing partnership with us.

Left: Monty and his daughter Princess Khaleesi – a natural bond that has emerged through herd living.

LIBERTY LOOSE SCHOOLING WITH THE COLTS
It is natural for us now to work with groups of ponies and encourage group learning – here are the four colts learning to work together at liberty.

Monsieur Chapeau and Dawn.

Monsieur Chapeau playing
peek-a-boo!

Monsieur Chapeau

Every Exmoor pony here is special – from magnificent stallion Bear to tiny late born foal Lady Martha of Molland Moor. However, particular acknowledgement must be given to Monsieur Chapeau. While the Exmoors generally are extremely adept at connecting with people if extended the right kind of treatment, he makes an extraordinary contribution to drawing interest in his breed. Since his rescue as an orphaned foal, he attracts a steady stream of visitors and his story has reached across the globe. He regularly meets and greets people with interest and curiosity and has an uncanny ability to understand what needs to be done and how to do it. He has an important role to play – whether helping to socialise foals, babysitting weanlings, connecting ponies within a herd, or people with ponies. His intuitive wisdom radiates across Holt Ball and we're forever grateful that he came into our lives.

Monsieur Chapeau's mother remains unidentified, so he remains unrecognised as an 'Exmoor pony' despite being a moorbred, purebred* Exmoor (*confirmed through DNA testing at Texas University and Monsieur Chapeau's sire was a registered Exmoor stallion). He is a constant reminder of the plight of similar moorland ponies and he motivates us to continue to work for improvement. He is also a reminder of the value of Exmoor pony geldings as ambassadors for the breed and why every effort should go into safeguarding the futures of colts too, along with the breeding stock.

Tribute to our treasured matriarch

The cycle of life brings joy and sorrow and, in the spring our beautiful mare Maisie increasingly lost condition, despite careful supplementary feeding and ad lib forage. She has always been what horse people describe as a 'good doer' looking marvellously well fed all year round. Further veterinary investigation confirmed our worst fears – Maisie tragically had cancer and nothing could be done about it. Nursing her through this last period, I sourced feeds and supplements that kept her comfortable and nourished until, at the beginning of June, it became clear that it was time for Maisie

to join the light. On the very afternoon that we made the sad decision, there was an incredible coincidence when artist Rebecca de Mendonca emailed me – out of the blue – a picture of a beautiful painting she'd been inspired to create after visiting us the previous summer. It was Maisie and her newborn foal Kilimanjaro! Rebecca has perfectly captured the essence of Maisie as the most wonderful, generous, powerful 'Earth Mother' and the light radiating in the painting has given me great comfort. Maisie was Bear's very first mare and it was a true and enduring love story for the two of them. It's been an honour to spend these years in the presence of her beautiful serenity and she will never be forgotten.

... and what of stallion Bear?

A wonderful new partnership has been created. Beautiful mare, Farleywater Scarlet Witch, who joined us as a moorbred foal from Buscombe in 2013 (along with Lady Stumpkin Pumpkin, Firestar and Dazzler) is now running with Bear. She has always caught my eye as a particularly good 'True Moorland Type' mare and she has the loveliest temperament. Anstey Princess completes Bear's small

Top, left to right: Monsieur Chapeau with Ruby, Alice, Cristabel and Clemmie Fraser; Monsieur Chapeau delighting his many fans at Christmas; with visitors and supporters Mark and Sue Summers.

Above left to right: Bethany Last and Monsieur Chapeau; Imperial Topaz meeting Katie Scorgie during a visit from the Society of Equestrian Artists; Exmoor Pony Project supporter Peter Hotchkiss with Lady Martha and Black Bess.

Matriarch until the last, Maisie centre here, flanked by Lady Molly and Penelope Pitstop – always central to activities.

Inset: Maisie and Kilimanjaro, painted by Rebecca de Mendonca.